Christ Our Life Series
Perform-a-Text

God Guides Us

This books belongs to
Lacy Karosic   LACY KAROSIC

Sister Jeanne Mary Nieminen, S.N.D.

Theological Advisors
Sister Agnes Cunningham, S.S.C.M.
Rev. Edward H. Konerman, S.J.

Consultant
Rev. Msgr. Joseph T. Moriarty

General Editor
Sister Mary Kathleen Glavich, S.N.D.

Loyola University Press
Chicago 60657

ISBN 0-8294-0550-4

©1987 Loyola University Press
Printed in the United States of America

Nihil Obstat Reverend Monsignor Joseph T. Moriarty, M.A.
     Censor Deputatus

Imprimatur Most Reverend Anthony M. Pilla, D.D., M.A.
     Bishop of Cleveland

     December 3, 1986

Acknowledgements

The general editor and the author wish to thank Sister Mary Raphaelita Böckmann, Sister Rita Mary Harwood, Sister Mary Dion Horrigan, and Sister Mary Nathan Hess, who have made the revision of this text possible. We would like to express appreciation to all who have inspired, prayed for, and encouraged us. Particular acknowledgement is due to Sisters Mary de Angelis Bothwell, Theresa Betz, St. Leo DeChant, Andrew Miller, Rita Mary Harwood and the other Sisters of Notre Dame who edited, planned, organized and wrote previous editions of *God Guides Us* as well as to the many catechists, parents, and others who evaluated the first editions and made valuable suggestions for this one. We also thank Sister Mary Catherine Rennecker who typed the manuscript and the Reverend Joseph F. Downey, S.J., Carol Tornatore, Ellen Scanlon, Chiara Padgett, Kristina Lykos, of Loyola University Press who transformed the manuscript into the attractive perform-a-text and manual.

This revision follows the guidelines of Pope John Paul II's Apostolic Exhortation "Catechesi Tradendae," *Sharing the Light of Faith: National Catechetical Directory for Catholics of the United States* and *To Teach as Jesus Did*. It implements the recommendations in the *Directory for Masses with Children, Rite of Christian Initiation of Adults, Moral Education and Christian Conscience* and *Respect Life Curriculum Guidelines* produced by the Department of Education, United States Catholic Conference.

Excerpts from the English translation of *The Roman Missal* © 1973; *Rite of Penance,* © 1974, International Committee on English in the Liturgy, Inc. All rights reserved.

Nicene Creed, taken from International
Consultation on English Texts

Songs are all in the public domain

Photos on page 170 by Art Resource/Scala, New York; page 144 by Camerique; page 111, 113 by H. Armstrong Roberts/Blumebild page 98, Metzen, page 166; page 158 by Historical Pictures Service-Chicago; pages 9, 17, 18, 46, 47, 57, 63, 69, 70, 86, 87, 94, 113, 115, 116, 117, 124, 173 by Ikonographics, Louisville Kentucky; page 172 by Allen Moore; pages 13, 23, 33, 66, 83, 98 by Jim and Mary Whitmer.

Illustrations by Ralph Smith and page 155, Sister George Ellen Holmgren, C.S.J.; also Arist Kirsch and Carol Tornatore.

Notes to Parents

Goals of the Program

This book of the revised *Christ Our Life* series presents to your child God's call to live with Him forever. The commandments are taught as signs of God's love and the beatitudes are introduced as Jesus' way to happiness. Your child is led to a greater appreciation of the sacraments and is encouraged to respond joyfully to God's call to live in the spirit of His love.

Format Designed to Make It a Family Program

You are urged to help your child evaluate his or her growth at the end of each unit by discussing with him or her the goals on page *iv*. Each week you are asked to review the perform-a-text pages for the theme covered in class. The pages that correspond to each theme are listed for you on the family pages at the beginning of each unit.

Each unit in the perform-a-text begins with a summary of the message that will be presented to your child in class. Usually a new theme is presented each week. The family pages at the beginning of the unit summarize the message of each theme and suggest related activities you can do as a family. Activities on the family pages are set up under four topics:

READ gives a scriptural reference related to what is presented in class. The reading can be done by a parent or older child in the family.

DISCUSS provides discussion starters that apply the scriptural reading to daily life.

PRAY sums up the message for the week in a prayer of the heart, a short prayer which everyone can say daily. This prayer could be printed and posted on the refrigerator or on a mirror. It could be added to meal prayers or other family prayers.

DO provides ideas for sharing at meals, playing word games, and enjoying family activities related to the message of the theme. Children's story books, available in public libraries, are suggested. Other books that convey the same truths may be substituted.

Educating Your Child to Live in Christ Jesus

After your child has completed a unit of study, guide him or her to consider the faith responses listed below. Let your child check each statement when he or she believes it has become a part of his or her Catholic Christian living. Sign your name on the line provided to show that you are aware of your child's efforts at growth in the areas that are listed below.

UNIT 1: God Calls Us to Be His, *pages* 1-37

_____ I am using my talents to bring joy to others.
_____ I know the Scripture quotes on pages 6 and 7 by heart.
_____ I can explain the five "Helps to Holiness" given on page 19.
_____ I can pray the rosary.

Parent's signature _____

UNIT 2: Jesus Is with Us on Our Way, *pages* 38-70

_____ I know the five ways given on page 45 to live the life of grace.
_____ I know the Prayer to the Holy Spirit and the Act of Contrition by heart.
_____ I examine my conscience every night.
_____ I receive the Sacrament of Reconciliation at least every few months.
_____ I am reverent when I receive Holy Communion.

Parent's signature _____

UNIT 3: We Keep God's Laws of Love, *pages* 71-132

_____ I pray every morning and evening.
_____ I honor God's name and all holy things.
_____ I celebrate Sunday by going to Mass and by trying to bring joy to others.
_____ I love, respect, and obey my parents and those who care for me.
_____ I show respect, care, and concern for all people, especially for babies, the sick, and the elderly.
_____ I respect the gifts of the earth by caring for them and by sharing them with others.
_____ I know the three rules given by St. Paul to help me be modest.
_____ I choose good friends and I am true to them.
_____ I tell the truth and keep my promises.
_____ I know the Ten Commandments by heart as they are given on page 81.

Parent's signature _____

UNIT 4: Jesus Leads Us to Happiness, *pages* 133-175

_____ I am satisfied with having only what I need.
_____ I pray and sacrifice for others and help those in need.
_____ I forgive those who hurt me and I pray for them.
_____ I do what is right, even when I must suffer for it.
_____ I do things that make for peace at home and I pray for peace throughout the world.
_____ I offer God a pure heart by praying the Morning Offering each day.

Parent's signature _____

Contents

		Page
Unit 1	**God Calls Us to Be His**	1
	Family Pages	2
1	God Calls Us	6
2	God Calls Us to Use Our Gifts	13
3	We Are God's Holy People	18
4	Mary Is Called to Be God's Mother and Ours	22
5	We Are Called to Follow Jesus	26
6	The Kingdom of Heaven Is Ours	32
Unit 2	**Jesus Is with Us on Our Way**	38
	Family Pages	39
7	God Shares His Wonderful Life of Grace	42
8	The Holy Spirit Lives within Us	46
9	God Blesses Contrite Hearts	50
10	God Forgives Us in the Sacrament of Reconciliation	55
11	God's Family Celebrates the Holy Eucharist	61
12	The Eucharist Is a Gift	66
Unit 3	**We Keep God's Laws of Love**	71
	Family Pages	72
13	We Learn About the Laws of God	78
14	We Show Our Love for God	83
15	We Love All That Is Holy	89
16	We Keep the Lord's Day Holy	93
17	We Honor and Obey	98

18	We Respect the Gift of Life	102
19	Jesus Showed Love and Concern for Others	107
20	We Are Faithful to Ourselves and Others	111
21	We Respect What God Has Given to Us and to Others	117
22	We Respect the Gifts of the Earth	120
23	We Speak the Truth with Love	124
24	We Keep God's Laws of Love	130

Unit 4 — Jesus Leads Us to Happiness — 133

	Family Pages	134
25	Happy Are the Poor in Spirit	138
26	God's Sorrowing and Lowly People Receive a Special Promise	145
27	God's People Long to be Pure of Heart and Holy	151
28	God's People Bring Mercy and Peace to Others	157
29	Jesus Leads Us to Happiness	163
30	We Rejoice with Mary	170

Liturgical Supplement

(Pages in parentheses are counted but not numbered because they are booklets or cut-outs.)

Mass Planning Sheet	176
Advent	(178)
Advent Tree	180
Lent	(182)
Morning Offering Prayer Cards	(184)
Joyful Mysteries Booklet	(186)
Sorrowful Mysteries Booklet	(188)
Glorious Mysteries Booklet	(190)
Confession Booklet	(192)

Unit 1 God Calls Us to Be His

The Message of the Unit

God calls each person to take part in His plan of salvation. The children are led to explore God's unique love for them and to discover the talents He has given them to fulfill that plan. Under the guidance of the Holy Spirit, they learn from Mary's example to respond willingly to God's call. They are challenged to follow Christ as His disciples, spreading the Good News as they travel toward their destiny — eternal happiness in heaven.

Sharing the Message as a Family

Family Pages for Themes in Unit 1

A mark in the box indicates that the theme has been presented in class.

Theme 1: ☐

God Calls Us, *pages* 6-12

God calls each of us to take part in His plan of salvation, and He promises His help and blessing if we trustingly respond to His call. Abraham and Ruth are models of fidelity to God's call. They show us that having faith means obediently doing whatever God asks, confident that He always brings us to a fuller, richer life when we faithfully follow His ways.

PRAY

Whenever you have something difficult to do, recall God's promise, "I have called you by name; you are Mine," and offer the work to Him.

DISCUSS

- What does this reading tell us about God's love?
- Does God promise to protect us from difficulties?
- What are the good things God has given your family?

READ Isaiah 43: 1-3

DO

- Memorize Isaiah 43:1.
- Make a photo collage of your family. Print around it the prayer from the book of Isaiah mentioned above. Ask your child to share with the family the story of Abraham and Ruth. After the story, discuss what each family member thinks was most difficult for Abraham and Ruth when they each heard God's call.
- Relate the difficulties experienced by Ruth and Abraham to those your family has experienced.

Theme 2: ☐

God Calls Us to Use Our Gifts, *pages* 13-17

Each person fulfills God's plan in a different way. To aid us in doing His will, God gives us the necessary gifts and talents. He expects us to be responsible for them: to develop them to the best of our ability, and to use them for His praise and glory, our own good, and the good of others.

READ Matthew 25: 14-30

DISCUSS

- What are the special talents God gave to each member of your family?
- How can these talents be used in the home?
- What type of job can each member perform to keep the family happy?
- How can each member use his or her talents to help the Church, the school, and the city in which we live?

DO

- Prepare a talent show for the family. Let each family member decide what he or she would like to do.
- Make gifts or tray favors for shut-ins and hospital patients.
- Plan to make home-made Christmas gifts for one another.
- Read the story of Johnny Appleseed and discuss how he used his talents for the good of many people.

PRAY

Whenever you use your talents to help someone else, offer the work to God and say:
ALL FOR YOU, MOST SACRED HEART OF JESUS!

Theme 3: ☐

We Are God's Holy People, *pages* 18-21

God calls us to be His holy people, and gives us His Son to be our Way, Truth, and Life. Jesus became man to show us how to live a holy life and to teach us the way to the Father. Through His Church, which is guided by the Holy Spirit, He continues to lead, strengthen, and form us into God's holy people.

DISCUSS

- How can we know what God is like?
- How does Jesus help us become God's holy people?
- How can the saints help us become holy? Name some saints.
- How can we help one another know God better? Love Him more? Serve Him well?
- Do you know anyone who is holy? Why do you think he or she is holy?

READ John 14: 6–9

DO

- Take turns telling something you know about Jesus. Continue until someone in the family has to pass.
- Plan to learn more about God by reading the Bible as a family a few minutes a day or some time during the week.
- Discuss whether or not your use of TV helps you to become more like Christ.
- Bring happiness to a sick or elderly friend by a cheerful visit.
- Ask your child to share the story of St. Francis. Some family members may want to help dramatize the play about St. Francis which appears on pages 20 and 21.

PRAY

As a reminder of our call to holiness, we will pray together:
HOLY FAMILY, MAKE OUR FAMILY HOLY.

Theme 4: ☐

Mary Is Called to Be God's Mother and Ours, *pages* 22-25

At the Annunciation, Mary was asked to be the mother of Jesus, God's Son. By saying *yes* she became our spiritual mother, the Mother of the Church, and of all people. We show our love for Mary by trying to answer God's calls willingly and promptly, as she did. We honor her in a special way by praying the rosary.

DISCUSS

- When did Mary become God's mother and ours?
- How did Mary answer God's call?
- How does God call us to do things for Him?
- How can we answer God's call as Mary did?
- When did God call you today and how did you answer?

READ
Luke 1: 26–33

PRAY

Think of how Mary responded to God's call and say:
HOLY MARY, MOTHER OF GOD,
PRAY FOR US SINNERS, NOW AND AT THE HOUR OF OUR DEATH.

DO

- Put Mary's picture or statue in a place for all to see.
- Each evening, gather around Mary's altar to pray the family rosary — or at least one decade.
- Make a rosary out of seeds, nuts, corn, cord, or flowers.
- Sing "Immaculate Mother," "Sing of Mary," or another song honoring Mary.
- Act out a mystery of the rosary, then pray that decade together.

Theme 5: ☐

We Are Called to Follow Jesus, *pages* 26-31

True disciples of Jesus listen to His words and walk in His way. They show their love for the Lord by sharing in His mission of leading all people to the Father.

READ
Luke 10: 1–2

DISCUSS

- What does Jesus ask us to do in this part of the Gospel?
- How do we show we are working for Jesus?
- What prayer will we say to ask God for more workers?

DO

- Make a prayer corner in your home to help you remember to pray for more workers for Jesus.
- Share with your child a time when a priest, deacon, brother, or sister helped you.
- Find out how many apostles each person in the family can name.
- Ask your child to tell the story about Jesus calling Saul to be His apostle.

PRAY

Try to follow Jesus as a true disciple by saying often each day:
WHAT AM I TO DO, LORD?

Theme 6: ☐

The Kingdom of Heaven Is Ours, *pages* 32-37

God has revealed to us our destiny, happiness with Him forever in heaven. Only then shall we see Him as He really is. In grateful response, we show our love for God by reaching out to others with love, and by striving to imitate Christ's acceptance of suffering.

READ
John 14: 1–9

DISCUSS

- Why does Jesus want us to trust in Him?
- What does Jesus tell us about heaven?
- What else do we know about heaven?
- What does Jesus mean when He says, "Whoever has seen Me has seen the Father"?

PRAY

Think of the joys of heaven and the way to get there. Pray together:

JESUS,
HELP US TO KNOW YOU MORE CLEARLY,
LOVE YOU MORE DEARLY,
FOLLOW YOU MORE NEARLY.

DO

- Have each member of the family tell how he or she imagines heaven will be. Then read St. John's account of his vision of heaven in Revelations 21:1–4.
- Decide what your family can do to follow Jesus — the Way, the Truth, the Life — more closely.
- Print *I am the Way, the Truth, the Life* on a card and post it near a crucifix, statue, or picture of Jesus.
- Have each family member write on slips of paper one or two good acts anyone in the family might do. Put the slips in a box and have each family member draw one. Consider each suggestion as a "Message from Jesus" and try to do what is suggested the following day. (Examples: Speak kindly, especially to family members. Help with the dishes. Don't complain today.)
- Have a family celebration or prayer service. Use the one on pages 35 and 36 or plan your own.
- Talk about the things you do — or don't do — just because you are a Christian trying to follow Jesus.

1 GOD CALLS US

God Calls Us by Name

"Hi, Marty!" "Tina!" "Mario!" Excited voices rang out as friends greeted each other after vacation.

Leah felt strange and alone. No one called her name. No one knew her. Then she heard "Leah!" She swallowed hard and looked up. Miss Link called out, "Boys and girls, this is Leah Flores. She's in our class this year. Leah came from Miami, Florida."
"Hi, Leah!" "Welcome, Leah!" friendly voices called from all parts of the room.

Leah smiled as she looked around. Everyone called her by name. Now she belonged.

When have you felt strange and alone? How do you feel when someone calls you by name?

What makes you feel you belong?

God calls each of us by name.
He knows us because He made us. We belong to Him.
God says,

"I have called you by name; you are mine."

Adapted from Isaiah 43:1

SMITH FAMILY

You belong to your family at home.
When you were baptized, you joined the Church.
Now you are called a Christian and a Catholic.
You belong to the big Christian family of people who believe in Jesus.
You also belong to the great human family of people all over the world.
All these families belong to God. He says,

"You will be my people and I will be your God."

Adapted from Leviticus 26:12

Draw a picture in the box to show a time when God called you by name.

You joined the family of Jesus, the Church, when you were baptized. Since then you have been called by two special names to show you belong to the Church. What are they? Print these names in the puzzle.

God Called Abram to Believe

Did you ever have to leave your home and move to a new one? How did you feel?

A long time ago God called a man named Abram. God said, "Leave your home, your country, and your family. Go to the land I will show you. I will make you the father of many people."

Abram did as God told him.
He went to the new land.
He believed that God would take care of him.

In the new land God spoke to Abram again and said, "You and your wife shall have a son. The children of your family will be as countless as the stars. You shall be called Abraham and your wife shall be called Sarah."

Abraham believed what God said.
He and Sarah had a son.
They called him Isaac.
He was a great joy to them.

Abraham always believed in God's loving care. He did what God asked, even when it was hard. God also calls us to believe in Him and to live with Him forever.

At Baptism we received the gift of faith. It helps us to believe in God. We know that He made us and that we belong to Him. We believe that He takes care of us in everything that happens.

Just as God spoke to Abraham, He speaks to us in our hearts. We can do what God tells us, even when it is hard. We can be happy with God forever.

WE REMEMBER

What does God call us to do?
God calls us to believe in Him and to do what He asks.

WE RESPOND

I walk in the presence of God;
In Him I trust.

Adapted from Psalm 56:13, 11

Abraham did what God asked because he had faith. We received the gift of faith at Baptism.
Do we do what God wants?

Imagine that the following things happen to you. Write what God calls you to say and do.

1. Your mother calls you when you are watching a favorite TV program. She wants you to clean your room.

   WHAT WILL YOU SAY? *ok mom*

   WHAT WILL YOU DO? *get up and clean my room*

2. Your teacher tells you to work a page in your math book for tomorrow. Math is hard for you and you don't want to do it. Your friend, who is very good at math, offers to let you copy his answers.

   WHAT WILL YOU SAY? *no I can do it myself*

   WHAT WILL YOU DO? *I'd do my paper*

Abraham did what God asked, even when it was hard.

Draw a picture of yourself doing something God asks you to do.

Check the family page for *Theme 1* on page 2.

God Called Ruth to Believe

Ruth lived in a country where people believed in false gods. Her husband and his mother, Naomi, told Ruth about God. When her husband died, Ruth lived with Naomi. She was kind to Naomi and helped her in many ways.

One day Naomi wanted to go back to her own country. Ruth loved her and wanted to go with her.
She said,

"I will go where you go.
 I will live where you live.
 I will love the God you love.
 I will belong to your people."

Ruth went with Naomi. In the new country, she worked and helped Naomi every day. She gathered grain in the fields.

One day, she met a good and kind man named Boaz. Ruth married him, and they were very happy together. God blessed them with a son. Ruth became the great-grandmother of King David. Into the family of David, many years later, the Savior was born.

2 GOD CALLS US TO USE OUR GIFTS

God Gives Us Special Gifts

Ms. Benson was returning the science booklets the children had made. She called Jenny. "You did excellent work, Jenny. Your cover is beautiful. You even wrote about six animals rather than four. You deserve this A."

As Joe came to her desk, Ms. Benson smiled. She praised him for the border of little animals he had drawn on the cover. Joe had done fine work in writing about each animal. Ms. Benson said he should be proud of the B+ he got on his book.

When Ms. Benson called Lottie, she did not look pleased. Lottie's cover was exactly like the sample Ms. Benson had shown. Lottie had even used the same colors. She had copied the paragraph about each animal from her science book. "I'm sorry, Lottie," Ms. Benson said, "I cannot give you a grade. You will have to make a new booklet."

Why was Ms. Benson pleased with Jenny and Joe?

Why couldn't Ms. Benson give Lottie a grade?

What will Lottie do?

13

Each one of us has a talent or something in us that makes us special. Underline the words in the blocks below that name your special abilities.

In the "What else?" section, write something special about you that is not shown. Then finish the sentences about yourself.

I like _acrobatics_.

I am good at _dancing_.

Something special about me is _reading_.

How can you use your talents to praise God and to help others?

David Used His Talents

Imagine that there were TV's in the time of David. Here are some pictures and stories that might have been on the news programs.

NEWS REPORT 1:
"Today David was taking care of his father's sheep, a job he does very well. Samuel visited the family and asked for David. He poured oil on David's head. This is a sign that God has chosen him to be our next king. David has the talents for this job. With God's help, he will be a good king."

NEWS REPORT 2:
"David uses the slingshot like a pro. That skill came in handy when David faced Goliath this afternoon. He struck the giant on the forehead with a stone. Goliath fell to the ground dead. David used his skill well. He gave glory to God and saved us from our enemies."

15

NEWS REPORT 3:

David was crowned king today. He takes the place of the late King Saul. David has a way of winning the love of all people. He said he has asked the Lord to stay with him and to rule with him. The people cheered when they heard this. They knew David would be a good king.

NEWS REPORT 4:

Last evening, David and the people held a celebration to thank God. They sang psalms of praise which David himself wrote. We can expect great things from a king who uses his talent to praise and love God.

Print the missing words in the puzzle below. The sentences and the WORD BANK will help you.

WORD BANK
God
Loves
Talent
Gifts
David

1. D A V I D
2. T A L E N T
3. L O V E S
4. G I F T S
5. G O D

1. A king who was anointed as a young boy is *David*.

2. A special ability is called a *talent*.

3. God made us special because He *loves* us.

4. Talents are special *gifts* from God.

5. We use our talents for *God* and others.

TODAY'S TV
Children
use their talents
to honor God
and to help
and give joy to others

WE REMEMBER

Why has God given me talents?
God has given me talents to praise Him
and to help others.

WE RESPOND

I will praise Yahweh all my life.

Adapted from Psalm 146:2

Check the family page for
Theme 2 on page 2.

17

3 WE ARE GOD'S HOLY PEOPLE

God Calls Us to Be Holy

When God our Father made us, He called us to be holy. He called us to know, love, and serve Him. He knows this is the way to happiness.

When Jesus came to earth, He showed us how to know, love and serve the Father. Jesus is still with us today in His Spirit and in His Church. He helps us answer God's call to become His holy people.

Holy people and _Saints_

Holy people living today and the saints in heaven help us to be holy.

The leaders of the Church teach us how to become holy.

Leaders

Sacraments and _Prayer_

When we meet Jesus in the sacraments and in prayer, He helps us to become holy.

Through the Bible, Jesus teaches us how to become holy.

Bible

Holy Spirit

Jesus sent the Holy Spirit to guide the Church and to help us become holy.

HELPS ON THE ROAD TO HOLINESS

1. Follow the path the boy and girl are walking. Read each sentence carefully. Find the word that names a "help to holiness." Print the word on the signpost nearest the sentence.
2. Trace the path and draw pictures of happy faces in the clouds.

St. Francis Answered God's Call

BROTHER FRANCIS (A Play)

CAST
Storyteller
Brother Francis
Brother Juniper
Birds (any number)
Brother Leo
Brother Bernard

Storyteller: One day, long ago, St. Francis and some of his friends were walking along a road.

Brother Bernard: Brother Francis, look at the field over there! It is filled with all kinds of birds.

Brother Francis: Yes, my brother. I must go see them.

Storyteller: St. Francis walked to the field. The birds did not fly away. Instead, they gathered around him. He knelt down and began to preach to them.

Brother Francis: My little ones, God made you and cares for you. You need not plant because He feeds you. He lets you build your nests in His trees. He gave you wings so that you could fly high in His sky. Your feathers keep you warm in winter. With your beautiful voices, you can praise Him for His goodness!

Storyteller: St. Francis stood up and blessed the birds with the Sign of the Cross. All the birds flew away, praising God with their songs.

Brother Juniper: Brother Francis, the birds seemed to understand what you told them.

Brother Francis: Yes, and they praised God for His goodness. God is good to us, too. He loves and cares for us even more than for the birds. God has called us to be holy. He sent His Son Jesus to show us how to know, love, and serve Him. We can be happy with Him some day in heaven.

Brother Leo: Let's praise God now for His goodness to us.

All the Brothers: Be praised, O God, for all Your goodness!

Brother Juniper: Bless us, too, Brother Francis.

Storyteller: St. Francis made the Sign of the Cross over his brothers. They went away with joyful hearts.

THE END

Check the family page for *Theme 3* on page 3.

WE REMEMBER

Who shows us how to be holy?
Jesus shows us how to be holy.
He helps us through His Spirit
and through the Church.

WE RESPOND

God chose us in Christ
to be holy and spotless
in his sight.

Adapted from Ephesians 1:4

4   MARY IS CALLED TO BE GOD'S MOTHER AND OURS

Mary Helps Us to Follow God's Call

Here is a poem that tells the story of Mary's call to be God's mother:

The Annunciation

In a town called Nazareth
So many miles away,
Mary hummed a melody
While at her work one day.

As she sang her songs of praise
An angel did appear.
"Do not be afraid, Mary,
Your God has sent me here.

"He has chosen you to be
The mother of His Son.
He will give His grace to you;
Just let God's will be done."

Mary said to Gabriel,
"With joy I'll do God's will."
Jesus' mother she became,
God's promise to fulfill.

God's own mother, Mary blest,
You are our mother, too.
Pray for us your children dear,
And make us just like you.

Mary answered God's call with words, "Yes, I will do as You will." She will help us do God's will also, if we ask her.

What might messengers of God tell us to do?

How can these boys and girls show that they have listened to God's messengers?

Color these words. We say them to God when we do what His messengers tell us.

23

Mary Calls Us to Pray the Rosary

Mothers like to receive handmade gifts from their children. Sometimes children pick flowers and make garlands or wreaths for their mothers.

Our mother Mary likes to receive a special garland from her children. This garland is the rosary. Its prayers are like a garland of roses. A story says that Mary gave the rosary to St. Dominic hundreds of years ago.

St. Dominic was a priest who loved our Blessed Mother and often prayed to her. One day he heard that some people were teaching things that were not true about God and His Son, Jesus. St. Dominic was worried that good Catholic people would believe these false teachings and lose the wonderful gift of faith.

Color the garland of flowers to make more beautiful.

Dominic prayed to Mary. He knew she would help. The story says that while he was praying, Mary appeared with a rosary in her hand. She said,

"Dominic, pray the rosary and teach the people to pray it."

The power of the rosary soon became known. Catholics grew stronger in their faith as they honored Mary. They believed what Jesus taught them through His Church.

Check the family page for *Theme 4* on page 4.

The Church reminds us to pray the rosary by naming October the Month of the Rosary, and by celebrating the Feast of the Holy Rosary on October 7. When we pray the rosary, we honor Mary and ask her to help us and all her children.

WE REMEMBER

Why do Catholics pray the rosary? Catholics pray the rosary to honor Mary and to know and love her Son Jesus more.

WE RESPOND

Hail Mary, full of grace, the Lord is with you.

5 WE ARE CALLED TO FOLLOW JESUS

Jesus Called Apostles

Jesus called some men to be His special followers. First He called two brothers, Peter and Andrew. He saw them fixing their fishing nets and called to them, "Come and follow Me. I will make you fishers of men! They left their nets and followed Jesus. Later Jesus called two more brothers, James and John.

Adapted from Mark 1:16-20

On another day, Jesus called Philip. Philip went to tell his friend, Nathanael, that he had found the Savior. Philip said, "He is Jesus, the son of Joseph from Nazareth." Nathanael could hardly believe it and asked, "Can anything good come from that town?" Philip said, "Come and see for yourself."

When Jesus saw Nathanael coming, He said, "Here comes a man who is honest." Nathanael was surprised. He asked, "How did You know me?"

Jesus explained, "Before Philip spoke to you, I saw you under the fig tree." Then Nathanael exclaimed, "Master, You are the Son of God!"

Adapted from John 1:43-49

Later Jesus called six other men to be His apostles. There were twelve in all. They came to believe that Jesus was the Son of God sent by the Father to save us. The apostles taught people the Good News. They healed the sick in His name. They became the first priests.

Find and circle 13 words that tell what Jesus' disciples do. The words go across and down.

```
L T R U S T P B S S
I C H E A U R T T A
S O T E A C A R E C
T B S T U D Y A A R
E E H E L P L S L I
N Y A T H A N K O F
F O R G I V E W V I
A R E P R A I S E C
L I E C H E A T R E
```

27

Jesus Called Some People to Be His Disciples

One day Jesus called other people to be His disciples. They were to help Him bring all people to God our Father. Jesus looked at a field of ripe grain. He said, "The field is full of grain, but there are only a few workers. Pray that God will send workers to gather in the harvest."

Adapted from Luke 10:1-2

That day Jesus chose seventy-two people to be His disciples. He told them to heal the sick and to teach the Good News that He had come to save them.
Jesus still calls people to follow Him today. He wants us to pray that more people become Christians. He wants us to pray for more priests, deacons, brothers, and sisters to serve His Church. Then He will have many helpers to spread the Good News of God's love.

WE REMEMBER

Whom does Jesus call to help Him spread the Good News of God's love?
Jesus calls all Christians to help Him spread the Good News of God's love.

WE RESPOND

"What am I to do, Lord?"

Acts 22:10

Work the puzzle. Use the clues and the WORD BANK.

Down:

1 People who believe in Jesus and follow Him are called _____.

2 Apostles and disciples of Jesus _____ people about Him.

Across:

3 Jesus wants to save all _____ from sin.

4 Priests, brothers, and sisters follow _____ in a special way.

5 Jesus told His disciples to _____ the sick.

WORD BANK

heal
teach
people
disciples
Jesus

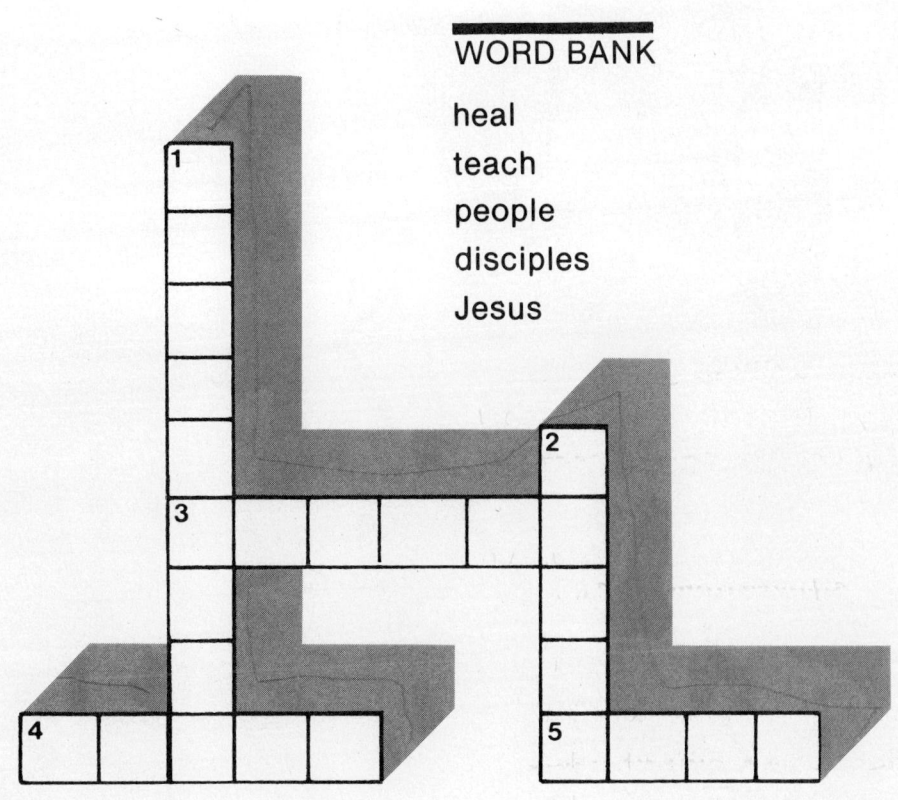

Saul Was Called to Be Paul

JESUS CALLED SAUL TO BE HIS APOSTLE   (A Play)

CAST	Reader	Jesus
	Saul	Ananias
	Friends

Scene I

Reader: Saul, along with some friends, was on his way to Damascus. He wanted to arrest people who followed the teachings of Jesus. Suddenly a great flash of light surrounded Saul. He fell to the ground. Then he heard a strange voice.

Jesus: Saul, Saul, why do you persecute Me?

Saul: Who are You, Sir?

Jesus: I am Jesus of Nazareth, and you are persecuting Me.

Saul: What am I to do, Lord?

Jesus: Stand up. Go into the city. There you will be told what you are to do.

(Jesus leaves. Saul, who has been blinded by the light, is led away by his friends.)

Scene II

Reader: Later Jesus appeared to a man named Ananias.

Jesus: Ananias, find the man named Saul who is praying and baptize him.

Ananias: Lord, that man hates Christians.

Jesus: It will be all right; I have chosen Saul to be My apostle.

(Ananias comes to Saul. He places his hands on Saul's head.)

Ananias: Brother Saul, the Lord Jesus has sent me. Receive your sight.

Saul: (Stands up.) I can see!

Ananias: God has chosen you to be His apostle. It is time you were baptized and had your sins washed away. Paul, call upon Jesus' name.

Saul: Jesus! Jesus!

Reader: Paul brought many people to Christ. He had to suffer much, but he suffered gladly because of His great love for Jesus.

Check the family page for *Theme 5* on page 4.

6 THE KINGDOM OF HEAVEN IS OURS

We Are Called to Be Happy with God Forever

JESUS HOME FOREVER HAPPY GOD LOVE LIFE HEAVEN JOY

Everyone wants to be happy.
God made us for happiness.
He knows we can be perfectly happy
only when we are with Him in heaven.
At the Last Supper Jesus said to His
apostles:

"I am going to leave you.
I am going to prepare a place
for you in My Father's house.
Some day I will come back
and take you with Me.
Then you will live with Me
forever.
You know the way to the place
where I am going."

Adapted from John 14:1-4

What is heaven like? St. Paul answers that question in the Bible:

"No one has ever seen or heard anything like it! No one can imagine what wonderful things God has prepared for those who love Him."

Adapted from 1 Corinthians 2:9

Heaven is our true home.
It is more beautiful and wonderful than we can imagine.
It is seeing God in all His beauty.
It is living in love with God forever.
It is joy, joy, joy!

Jesus Is the Way to Eternal Life

Once a rich young man asked Jesus, "What must one do to live with God forever?"

Jesus said, "Keep the commandments." The man told Jesus, "I have kept all these. What else can I do?"

Then Jesus answered, "If you want to prove your love, go and sell all you have. Give the money to the poor. Then come and follow Me. You will have treasure in heaven."

Adapted from Mark 10:17-21

WHAT ARE SOME OF THE TREASURES IN HEAVEN?

Name four of them on the lines below. Use the WORD BANK.

_____
_____
_____
_____
_____
_____
_____
_____

WORD BANK
FUN
ANGELS
FRIENDS
BEAUTY
PEACE
MARY
GOD
JOY

Check the family page for *Theme 6* on page 5.

WE REMEMBER

What is the way to eternal happiness? The way to eternal happiness is to know, love, and serve God in this world.

WE RESPOND

As a deer longs for running streams, so my soul longs for you, my God.

Psalm 42:1

34

The Joys of Heaven Last Forever

SONG: JULIE'S PSALM

Let us sing a song to our Father,
As we walk along to our Father.
He is always there,
God is taking gentle care;
God is love beyond compare,
God is good.

To His home above He leads me,
With His gift of peace He frees me.
High on angel wings,
My heart gives Him thanks and sings:
How He fills us with good things!
God is good.

READING: *Matthew 6:19-21*

PSALM PRAYER:

How lovely is Your home on high,
O Lord, our God!
My heart is filled with longing
To see Your house, O Lord.

Happy are they who live in Your home.
They praise You all day long.
Happy are they who trust in You;
They shall see You face to face.

Adapted from Psalm 84

A MESSAGE FROM JESUS

I want you to think of Me and the joys I promise you in heaven.

LITANY OF JOY

Response: We thank You, Jesus.

Jesus, You show us the way to Your Father's house.
You gave us Mary as our Heavenly Mother.
You gave us a beautiful world to help us think of You.
You gave us one another.
You teach us that the joys of heaven are the greatest of all.
You promise treasure in heaven that will last forever.

SONG: WHEN THE SAINTS GO MARCHING IN
Adapted from the Spiritual

O when the saints go marching in,
O when the saints go marching in,
O I want to march beside them
When the saints go marching in.

O when the saints give praise to God,
O when the saints give praise to God,
O I want to sing beside them
When the saints give praise to God.

God Calls Us to Be His

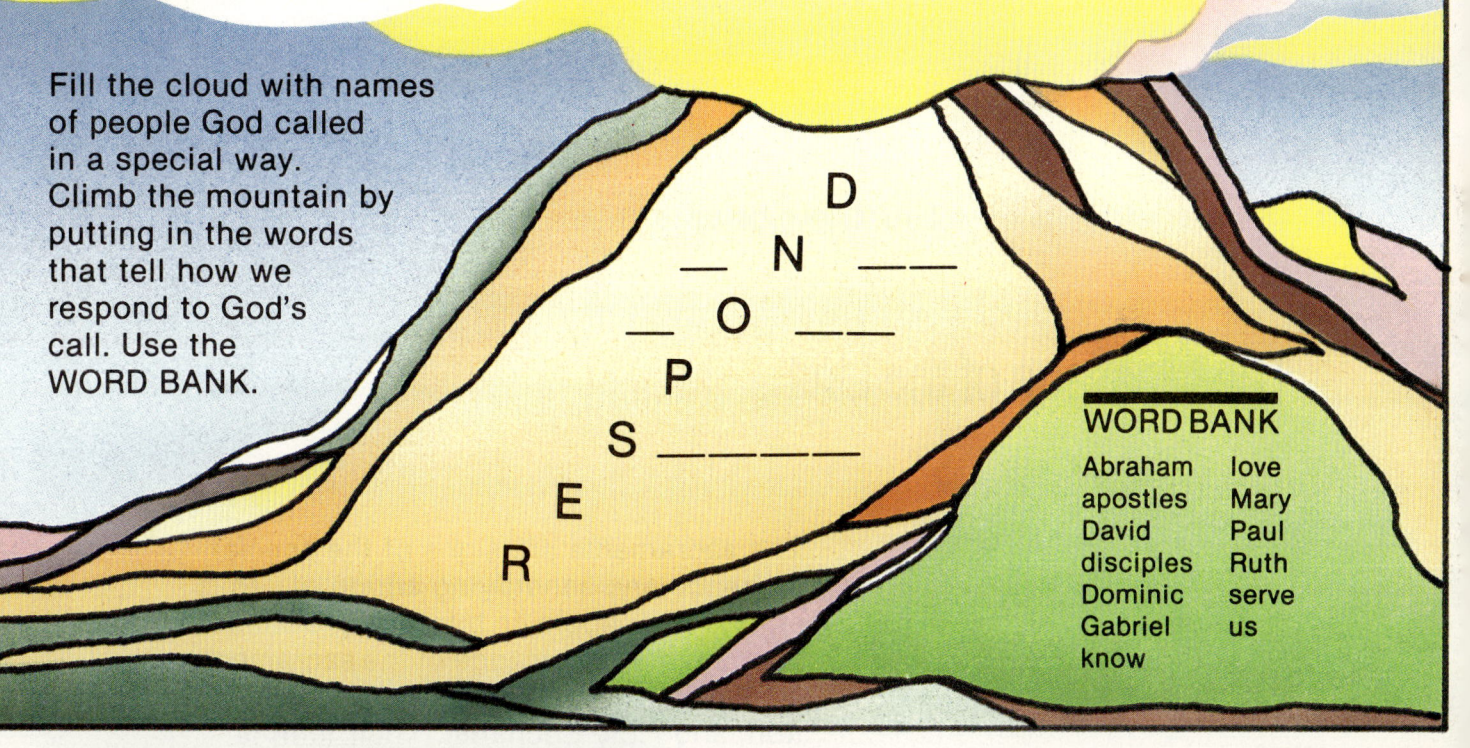

R_TH   _P_STL_S
G_BR___L   P___L
    M_RY   D_SC_PL_S
_BR_H_M   D_V_D
    _S   D_M_N_C

Fill the cloud with names of people God called in a special way. Climb the mountain by putting in the words that tell how we respond to God's call. Use the WORD BANK.

```
            D
        _ N _ _
      _ O _ _
      P
    S _ _ _ _
  E
R
```

WORD BANK

Abraham   love
apostles   Mary
David   Paul
disciples Ruth
Dominic   serve
Gabriel   us
know

A SECRET MESSAGE FROM GOD

See if you can find 33 squares of this size: ☐ Color them black to find God's message.

Unit 2 Jesus Is With Us on Our Way

The Message of the Unit

The sacraments are signs of the special presence and sanctifying action of Jesus among His people. In this unit, the children deepen their knowledge of the sacraments, especially those of Baptism, Reconciliation, and Holy Eucharist. Their faith is deepened as they gain a better understanding of the sacramental effects on themselves and on the whole family of God. They are motivated to frequent reception of the Sacraments of Reconciliation and Holy Eucharist, and are guided to assist at Mass with greater understanding, eagerness, and love.

Sharing the Message as a Family

Family Pages for Themes in Unit 2
A mark in the box indicates that the theme has been presented in class.

Theme 7: ☐ God Shares His Wonderful Life of Grace, *pages* 42-45

Because of His great love for us, God sent His only Son to suffer and die so that we might share in His life. This life of grace was given to us in Baptism. Through this sacrament, God dwells in us and enables us to live as His children. We can grow in grace through prayer, the sacraments and by trying to lead a good Christian life.

DISCUSS
- What kind of man was Nicodemus?
- How did Jesus describe Baptism to Nicodemus?
- Why is water such a meaningful sign of Baptism? (Consider some of the uses of water.)
- How did Jesus earn the grace we receive in Baptism?

READ
John 3: 1-17

DO
- Have a "Baptismal Anniversary" celebration for each member of the family.
- Light the baptismal candle and have all members of the family renew their baptismal promises.
- If there is a new member in your family or in the family of a relative or friend, make the white robe or provide the candle for the Baptism.
- Talk about how you as a family are living your life of grace. Use page 45.

PRAY
As a reminder of the wonderful Sacrament of Baptism, say:
LET THY SAVING WATERS FLOW OVER US, O LORD.

Theme 8: ☐ The Holy Spirit Lives within Us, *pages* 46-49

The Holy Spirit helps us, through His gifts, to do good and avoid evil. He leads us to reflect the image of the Lord, each according to his or her gifts, until we are changed into the image of Jesus. This, then, is the will of God—our sanctification.

DISCUSS
- What is meant by the "brightness" of Jesus?
- In what ways can we reflect this "brightness"?
- How does the Holy Sprit help us become more like Jesus?
- What can we do to cooperate with the Holy Spirit?
- How can we help one another reflect the goodness of Jesus?

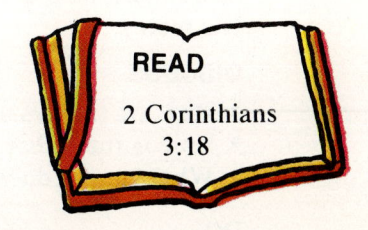

READ
2 Corinthians 3:18

PRAY
Each time you look in a mirror, remember that you should reflect Jesus and say:
HOLY SPIRIT, MAKE ME LIKE JESUS.

DO
- Have members of the family think of various ways of reflecting Jesus. Use the "map" on page 48 for ideas. Family members might like to role-play or act out situations which provide an opportunity for following the Holy Spirit.
- In order to learn more about Jesus, plan to read about His life in the Gospels. You might do this as a family a few minutes a day or on a certain day of the week before the evening meal.
- Ask your child to tell the story of St. Dominic Savio to the family.

Theme 9: God Blesses Contrite Hearts, *pages* 50-54

Jesus loves us with a forgiving love. No matter what our sins or sinfulness, He is always ready to reconcile us with Himself and the Father if we are sorry. We need but to trust in Him and allow His love to help us change our lives.

READ Luke 7: 36-50

DISCUSS
- How did the sinful woman show her love for Jesus?
- What example did Jesus give Simon to show that the more we are forgiven, the more we love?
- Why did Jesus forgive the sins of the woman?
- Why is it sometimes hard for us to forgive?

PRAY
Think of the many times Jesus has forgiven your sins and say:
THANK YOU, JESUS, FOR YOUR FORGIVING LOVE.

DO
- Make a chain of acts of love to God by forgiving others when they hurt you.
- Discuss symbols of sorrow, peace, and reconciliation. Put them on a banner to be displayed in your home.
- Hang a crucifix or picture of Jesus in your house to remind the family of God's presence in your home.
- Renew the practice of the examination of conscience before retiring.
- Have your child tell the family about St. Peter's sin and sorrow.
- Read about St. Philip Neri, who was able to bring sinners to God by his humor and common sense.

Theme 10: God Forgives Us in the Sacrament of Reconciliation, *pages* 55-60

God is a loving and forgiving Father. Though we reject His love when we sin, He is always ready to welcome us when we return to Him in the Sacrament of Reconciliation. In receiving the Sacrament, we must express sorrow for our offenses and trust in His mercy.

READ Luke 15: 11-32

DISCUSS
- How are the five steps for receiving the Sacrament of Reconciliation shown in this story?
- How is the father in the story like God, our heavenly Father?
- What can we do when we feel unforgiving toward others?

DO
- Plan and conduct a family reconciliation service.
- Do some planning to make the day a joyful one for a member of the family who may be receiving the Sacrament of Reconciliation for the first time.
- Tell the story of the forgiving father and the lost son with a "paper movie."
  (To make this "movie," draw a series of pictures on shelf-lining paper or similar material. Tell the story as you show the pictures.)
- If you have some broken or forgotten friendships, decide what definite steps you should take to renew them.

PRAY
Each evening, after an examination of conscience, pray:
LORD, HAVE MERCY ON ME, A SINNER

Theme 11: ☐ **Jesus Stays with Us in the Holy Eucharist,** *pages* 61-65

The great love of Jesus is shown by His institution of the Holy Eucharist at the Last Supper. The sacrifice He offered for us through His death on the Cross is renewed daily in the Holy Sacrifice of the Mass. By participating in the Eucharistic Sacrifice and by making visits to the Blessed Sacrament, we grow in love for Him and for one another.

DISCUSS

- Why did Jesus give us Himself in the Holy Eucharist?
- Why did Jesus suffer and die for us?
- How does the Mass help us remember Jesus' sacrifice?
- How can we thank Jesus for the Holy Eucharist?

READ Matthew 26: 26-29

PRAY

When going into the Church, say:
O SACRAMENT MOST HOLY, O SACRAMENT DIVINE,
ALL PRAISE AND ALL THANKSGIVING BE EVERY MOMENT THINE.

DO

- Make a family mobile of symbols of the Holy Eucharist and Mass.
- Prepare for Sunday Mass as a family. Read and discuss the Scripture readings if possible; decide how best to participate at Mass; prepare for receiving Jesus in the Holy Eucharist.
- Have each member of the family write a short prayer thanking Jesus for His presence in the Holy Eucharist. Share the prayers in a little thanksgiving celebration or as part of grace after meals.
- Make a visit to Church to thank Jesus for being with us in the Blessed Sacrament.

Theme 12: ☐ **Jesus Makes Us One through the Mass,** *pages* 66-70

Jesus prays that all who gather in love and as one family to share the meal of the Holy Eucharist will be one with Him and with one another. That we may grow in this unity, He offers Himself to the Father and comes to us in Holy Communion.

DISCUSS

- What did Jesus call Himself?
- Where did the Living Bread come from?
- What does Jesus promise to those who eat this Bread?
- When do we receive this Living Bread?
- How can we show Jesus that we appreciate His gift to us?

READ John 6:51-58

PRAY

At grace before meals, pray together:
LORD, THANK YOU FOR THE BREAD TO FEED OUR BODIES,
AND FOR THE LIVING BREAD TO FEED OUR SOULS.

DO

- Think of an especially happy family meal. Discuss it in regard to food, people present, conversation, and occasion. How did it help you grow closer as a family?
- Compare the family meal with the Eucharistic meal. How are they alike or different?
- Make placemats for the family table. Decorate them with drawings or magazine pictures of wheat, grapes, chalice, or other symbols of the Holy Eucharist.
- Have each family member suggest ways to make mealtime happy and pleasant.
- Plan to make one Sunday of the month a "Family Communion Sunday," when all family members can attend the same Mass and receive Holy Communion together.

7 GOD SHARES HIS WONDERFUL LIFE OF GRACE

Jesus Brings Us a Share in God's Life

God loved the first people He made very much. He wanted them to enjoy a close friendship with Him. So He shared His God life, or grace, with them. He made them God-like so that they belonged to His family.

But Adam and Eve had the power to choose. They refused God's friendship. They chose to disobey God. They sinned. They lost grace and were no longer God's children.

We call this first sin original sin. It brought all kinds of evil into God's good world. It lost God's life of grace for all of us. Now people are born without God's life of grace.

Adam and Eve were sorry for what they had done. They were not happy in their sin. God's love for us was so great that He sent His own Son, Jesus, to save us from sin. Because Jesus died for us, we can share in God's life again. We can belong to God's family as His children. We can live with Him forever in heaven.

WORD CHOICE

Underline the word or phrase that completes each sentence.

1. God gave His life to Adam and Eve so that they would (be as great as He is, be His children, not obey Him).
2. God sent (Adam and Eve, Mary, Jesus) to save us from sin.
3. We are born in original sin, which means without (our sight, good health, the life of grace).
4. Our share in God's life is called (love, grace, hope).

We Receive the Life of Grace in Baptism

An important man named Nicodemus came to Jesus and said, "You are a teacher. You have come from God. No one can do the things you do. God is with You."

Jesus told him, "You must be born of water and the Spirit to enter God's kingdom." "How can that be possible?" asked Nicodemus. Jesus was talking about Baptism. Through His death on the cross, Jesus gives God's life in Baptism to those who believe in Him. Jesus said,

"God loved the world so much that He sent His only Son, so that everyone who believes in Him may have eternal life."

Adapted from John 3:16

Most of us were baptized when we were little babies. Our parents and godparents took us to church. They promised to help us live as Christians.

Then the priest baptized us with water. He called us by name and said: "I baptize you in the name of the Father, and of the Son, and of the Holy Spirit."

These words and the water are the signs used in the Sacrament of Baptism. When the priest used them, sin was taken away. Jesus gave us His life of grace. We became united with Him. He welcomed us into His family, the Church. Now we can live as God's children on earth. We can live with God in heaven forever.

A PUZZLE ON BAPTISM

Make other words using some of the letters in the word BAPTISM. The sentences and WORD BANK will help you.

1. In Baptism we receive a share in _____ _ _ _ _ _ God's life called _____.

2. _ _ _ _ _ _____ is poured on us when we are baptized.

3. The grace we receive in Baptism _____ _ _ _ _ is new _____.

4. _____ _ _ _ _ _ _____ told us that we can live with Him if we are baptized.

WE REMEMBER

What does Baptism do for us? Baptism gives us new life in Jesus. We become members of the Church and children of God.

WE RESPOND

Give thanks to the Lord, for He is good, His love is everlasting.

Adapted from Psalm 118:1

Check the family page for *Theme 7* on page 39.

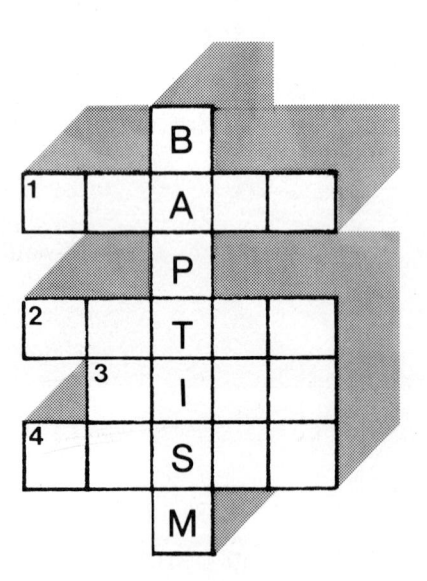

WORD BANK
Water
Life
Grace
Jesus

We Live the Life of Grace

FOLLOW THE PUZZLE PATH

Start with the letter "P" at the bottom of the PUZZLE PATH.

Circle every other letter to find the words that complete the sentences. They will tell you how you can live your life of grace and grow as the child of God.

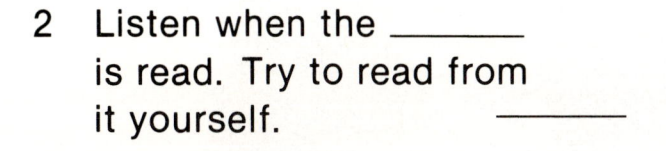

1 _____ every day.

2 Listen when the _____ is read. Try to read from it yourself.

3 Receive Jesus in Holy _____.

4 Obey God's _____.

5 _____ the gifts God has given you.

The sacraments are special ways in which God shares His life with us. Match the name of a sacrament (BAPTISM, HOLY EUCHARIST, RECONCILIATION) with each picture below:

_____   _____   _____

45

8 THE HOLY SPIRIT LIVES WITHIN US

The Holy Spirit Leads Us to Do Good

The Holy Spirit lives within us since our Baptism.
He makes us more like Jesus.
St. Paul tells us:
"Like mirrors we reflect the brightness of the Lord. We grow brighter and brighter as we are changed into the image of Jesus. This is the work of the Holy Spirit."

Adapted from 2 Corinthians 3:18

The Holy Spirit shares with us His own goodness and leads us to heaven.

faith

kindness

Come, Holy Spirit,
fill the hearts
of Your faithful,
and kindle in them
the fire of Your love.

peace

_____ patience _____

Read the words near the dove that tell the good things the Holy Spirit shares. Each picture shows a gift from the Holy Spirit. On the line under each picture, name the gift it shows.

Faith
Generosity
Joy
Patience
Peace
Love
Kindness

_____ love _____

_____ joy _____

47

The Holy Spirit Helps Us Avoid Evil

Jesus gave us the Holy Spirit. With His help we can overcome temptations and avoid sin. St. Paul says, "If you let the Holy Spirit lead you, you will not be selfish.

People who are selfish become enemies. They fight and argue. They hurt themselves and others.

If the Spirit leads you, you will be full of love, joy, peace, kindness, and goodness.

Since the Spirit has given us life, let us be led by Him."

Adapted from Galatians 5:16,19,25

The Holy Spirit helps us to be truly wise. To be wise means to know what is good and what is evil. If we listen to the Holy Spirit, we will know what is right. We will be able to say *No* to temptation and sin. We will be able to do what is good.

The Holy Spirit gives us special help when we pray and celebrate the sacraments.

This is a road map from Old Town to New Town. Color all the roads the Spirit would tell you to take.

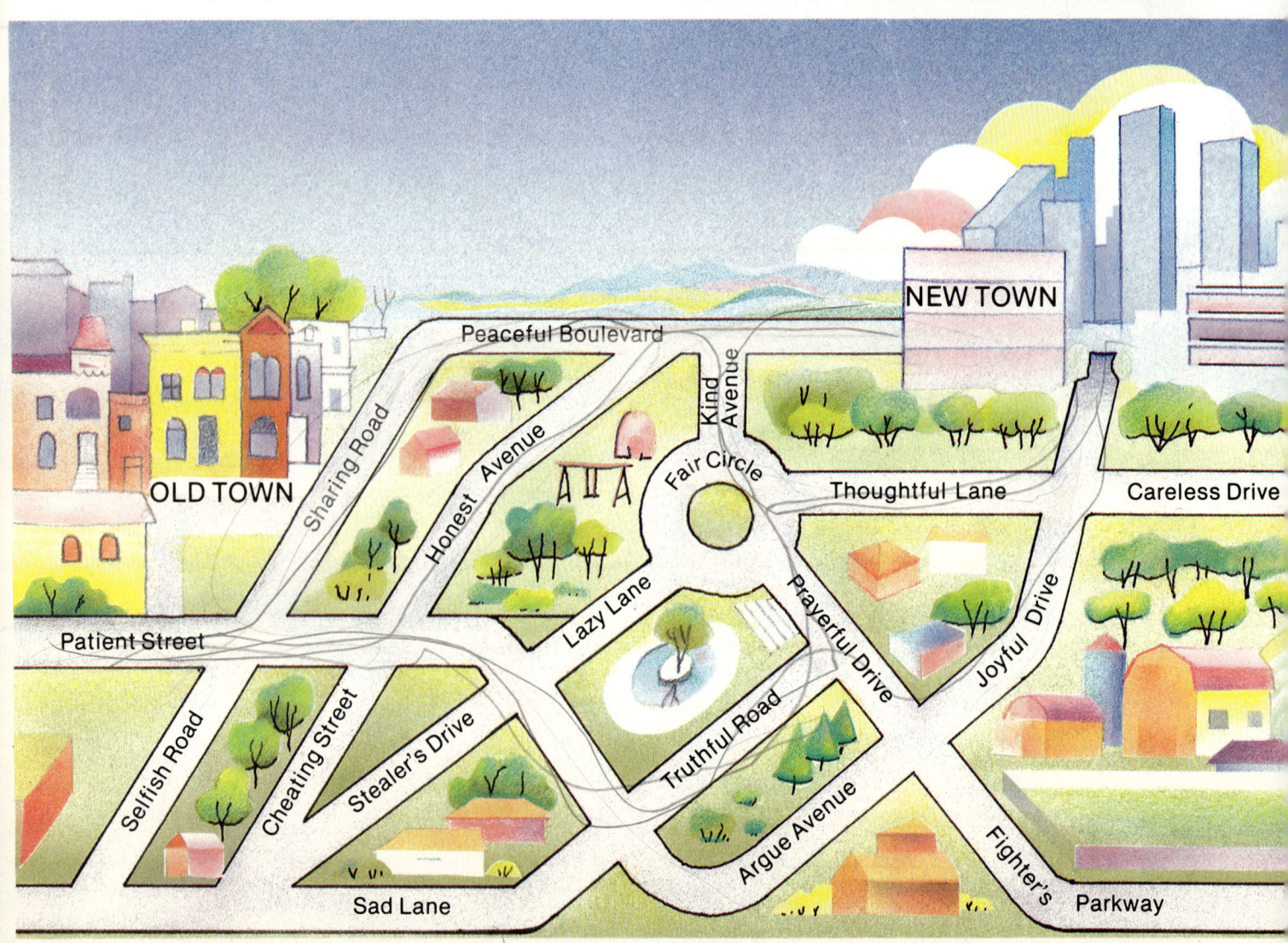

Complete the sentence under each picture. Use the WORD BANK.

WORD BANK
pray
Reconciliation
Communion

The Holy Spirit helps us know what is good when we _____ _____ _____.

When we receive Holy _____ _____, the Holy Spirit fills us with grace.

When we celebrate the Sacrament of _____ _____ _____, the Holy Spirit helps us say *No* to sin.

WE REMEMBER

What is sin?
Sin is choosing to think, say or do what we know offends God and what may also hurt ourselves and others.

WE RESPOND

Come, Holy Spirit, fill the hearts of Your faithful, and kindle in them the fire of Your love.

Check the family page for *Theme 8* on page 39.

9 GOD BLESSES CONTRITE HEARTS

Jesus Forgave Peter

At the Last Supper Jesus looked at Peter and said, "Simon, the devil will tempt you. But I have prayed that your faith will not fail." Peter loved Jesus very much and promised, "Lord, I will go to prison with You and die with You." Jesus knew that Peter was not strong enough to do that. He warned him and said, "Peter, before the rooster crows today you will three times deny that you know Me."

After the supper, Jesus and the apostles went to a garden to pray. When they arrived, Jesus said, "Pray that you will not give in to temptation." Then He went a little farther into the garden and prayed to His Father. When He came back, the apostles were asleep. He said to them, "Why are you sleeping? Get up and pray that you will not give in to temptation."

As Jesus spoke, a crowd of soldiers came and arrested Him. They took Him away to judge Him. Peter followed them but stayed a little behind.

A servant girl looked at Peter and said, "You were with Jesus." Peter answered, "No, I do not know Him."

After a while a man noticed Peter and said, "You are one of His friends." But again Peter answered, "No, sir, I am not!"

About an hour later another man saw Peter and said, "You were surely with Jesus. You even talk like He does." Again Peter said, "No, I do not know what you are talking about."

While he was speaking, the rooster crowed. Just then, Jesus passed by as He went to prison. He turned and looked at Peter. Peter remembered the Lord's words.

Peter went out and wept with great sorrow. Jesus, Who still loved Peter very much, saw his sorrow and forgave him completely.

Adapted from Luke 22:31-34, 39-46, 54-62

ACT OF CONTRITION

My God, I am sorry for my sins with all my heart. In choosing to do wrong and failing to do good, I have sinned against you whom I should love above all things.

I firmly intend, with your help, to do penance, to sin no more, and to avoid whatever leads me to sin.

> Write the parts from the Act of Contrition that tell:

■ how you have sinned *In choosing to do wrong and failing to do good.*

■ against whom you have sinned *God*

■ what you promise to do *To avoid sin.*

God's Word Tells of His Forgiving Love

THE TWO MEN IN THE TEMPLE

Two men went up to the temple to pray. The first man thought of the good things he had done and prayed, "I thank You, O God, that I am not like other people—dishonest, unfair, and unkind. I thank You that I am better than this tax collector."

The other man knelt behind the first man. He thought of the times he had kept all of God's commandments. He said, "Lord, have mercy on me, a sinner." God was pleased with the second man because he was sorry. This man went home with God's peace, but the other did not.

Adapted from Luke 18:10-14

JESUS AND THE SINFUL WOMAN

One day a man named Simon, who wanted to know more about Jesus, invited Him to his house for a meal. While Jesus and the other guests were eating, a woman came into the room. She was sad because she had not always kept God's laws of love. She came to tell Jesus that she was sorry.

The sinful woman went right up to Jesus and knelt down. She washed Jesus' feet with her tears. She used her long hair to dry them. Jesus looked at her and loved her. He was pleased that she was sorry.

Simon did not like this. He thought Jesus should not let a sinner touch Him. Jesus knew what Simon was thinking and said, "This woman's sins must have been forgiven, or she would not show such great love."

Then Jesus spoke to the woman and said, "Your sins are forgiven. Go in peace." The woman's heart was filled with peace and joy.

Adapted from Luke 7:36-50

THE SHEPHERD AND HIS LOST SHEEP

A man had a hundred sheep. One ran away and got lost. The shepherd loved the lost sheep just as he loved all the sheep in his flock. Because he knew the others were all right, he left the ninety-nine and went to look for the lost one. He searched everywhere until he found it. Then he lifted it up, and with great joy carried it back to the flock.

When he got home, he invited his friends and neighbors to celebrate with him. He said, "Rejoice with me, because I have found my lost sheep."

In the same way, there is great joy in heaven whenever anyone is sorry for his or her sins.

Adapted from Luke 15:4-7

JESUS AND ZACCHAEUS

One day Jesus was passing through the town of Jericho. A rich man named Zacchaeus was so short that he could not see Jesus. So he climbed a tree and sat on one of the branches. When Jesus saw him, He said, "Zacchaeus, hurry down, for I must stay at your house today."

Zacchaeus hurried down and welcomed Jesus with great joy. Some of the people started to grumble and say, "Jesus has gone to the house of a sinner." But Zacchaeus was sorry for cheating the people. He told Jesus, "I will give half of my belongings to the poor. If I have cheated anyone, I will pay him back four times as much."

Jesus was pleased and said, "The blessing of God has come to this house today."

Adapted from Luke 19:1-10

We Think of God and His Forgiving Love

Jesus is with us always in His Holy Spirit because He loves us. He speaks to us and reminds us to love Him and others. We examine our conscience to find out how we have loved God and others. We ask ourselves how we have kept God's commandments. When we admit our failings and are sorry for them, God blesses us with His peace. A daily examination of conscience will help us remember God's presence. We will come to love God and others more.

EXAMINATION OF CONSCIENCE

1. Have I remembered to speak to God in prayer each morning and evening? How attentively have I prayed?

2. Have I always used God's name with love and respect?

3. Have I taken part in the Eucharist with God's family to celebrate Sundays and Holy Days? Was I on time? How well did I pray and sing? How else did I celebrate Sunday?

4. Have I obeyed my parents and others in authority when I was told to do what God wants? How have I shown them love and respect by my words and actions?

5. How have I taken care of the gift of life, my health and that of others? Do I show respect for my body? Do I show respect for others?

6. Have I used the gifts and talents God has given me to serve Him and others? How kind have I been to the members of my family? To other children? To the poor, the old, and the handicapped?

7. How well have I taken care of the things God has given to me to serve Him and others? Have I shared with those in need?

8. Have I always spoken the truth? Have I kept secrets and promises? Have my words been kind? Have I spoken up for what is right?

WE REMEMBER

When does God forgive us?
God forgives us when we are
sorry for our sins.

WE RESPOND

I am sorry for my sins with all my heart.

from Act of Contrition

Check the family page for *Theme 9* on page 40.

10 GOD FORGIVES US IN THE SACRAMENT OF RECONCILIATION

A Father Forgives His Son

One day Jesus told this story about a father who forgave his lost son:

Reader: Once there was a rich man who had two sons. One day, the younger son came to his father and said:

Son: Father, give me a share of the money. I am tired of living at home. I want to see some new things.

Father: I am sorry that you want to leave home, but here is the money.

Reader: The son was happy at first. He spent his money having good times with his friends. When the money ran out, his friends left him. He had to find work because he had nothing to eat. The only job he could get was feeding pigs. Even then he was hungry most of the time. One day, he sat down to think about what he had done.

Son: What have I done? I have hurt my father. I have hurt myself.

Reader: Then he began to feel sorry for the way he had behaved.

Son: I am so sorry that I hurt my father. He worked so hard for that money.

Reader: He tried to decide what he should do about it.

Son I know what I will do. I will go back to my father. I will never be so selfish again. I will try to please my father.

Reader: He tried to think of what to say to his father.

55

Son: I will tell my father what I have done. I will tell him I am sorry.

Reader: He wanted to do something to make up to his father for what he had done.

Son: I will do anything he wants. I will work as a servant in his house.

Reader: He went home. His father saw him coming and ran to meet him. He put his arms around him and welcomed him.

Son: Father, I am sorry.

Father: Welcome home, my son. You are forgiven. Come, we must celebrate!

Adapted from Luke 15:11-24

Like the son in the story, we ask our Father's forgiveness when we celebrate the Sacrament of Reconciliation.

Draw a picture of yourself telling God you are sorry.

We Prepare for the Sacrament of Reconciliation

Jesus loves us, even when we fail to love Him and others. He forgives our sins when we are sorry. He forgives us in the Sacrament of Reconciliation.

I ask the Holy Spirit to help me celebrate this sacrament.

*Come, Holy Spirit, help me
look into my heart.
Show where I have failed
to love God and others.
Help me to be sorry.
Help me to grow in God's life.
Amen.*

I examine my conscience to find out how I have sinned in my thoughts, in my words, in my actions, or in what I have failed to do. I pray an Act of Contrition to tell God that I am sorry. I ask God to help me love Him and others more.

When I celebrate the Sacrament of Reconciliation, I meet Jesus. I meet Him through the priest who hears my confession.

1. The priest welcomes me. I greet him.
2. I make the Sign of the Cross and tell how long it has been since my last confession.
3. I listen to the priest's prayer and Scripture reading.
4. I tell my sins. I may tell the priest any problems I have living as a Catholic.
5. I listen to the priest. He gives me a penance to make up for my sins.
6. I pray an Act of Contrition.
7. When the priest gives me absolution, I make the Sign of the Cross.
8. The priest says, "Give thanks to the Lord, for he is good." I answer, "His mercy endures forever."
9. The priest may say something like: "Goodbye. God love you." I say: "Thank you, Father" and leave.
10. I thank God for His forgiving love and peace. I ask the Holy Spirit to help me live as God's loving child. I do the penance the priest gave me. If it is a prayer, I pray it right away. If it is a deed, I do it as soon as I can.

CLIMB THE PEACE TREE

Fill in the missing words. Use the WORD BANK.

WORD BANK

Promise
Make up
sorry
confession
Examine
God's loving children

6. Live as _God's loving children_
5. _make up_ for your sins.
4. Go to _confession_
3. _Promise_ to do better.
2. Be _sorry_
1. _Examine_ your conscience.

WE REMEMBER

What does Jesus do for us in the Sacrament of Reconciliation? Jesus forgives us and gives us His peace and love in the Sacrament of Reconciliation.

WE RESPOND

Give thanks to the Lord, for He is good. His mercy endures forever.

Adapted from Psalm 118:1

Check the family page for *Theme 10* on page 40.

59

Jesus Forgives Us

Finish the PEACE FLAG by printing in the missing words. Use the WORD BANK.

P When we tell God we will do better, we make a _Promise_.
E When we tell our sins to the priest, we _Confess_ them.
A When we carefully look over what we have done, we _examine_ our conscience.
C Jesus loves _contrite_ hearts.
E The priest gives us a _penance_ to make up for our sins.

Finish the PEACE FLAG by printing in the missing words. Use the WORD BANK.

	P					
P	R	O	M	I	S	E
C	O	N	F	E	S	S
	e	X	A	M	I	N	E
	a		C	O	N	T	R	I	T	E
	c					
P	E	N	A	N	C	E

WORD BANK
CONFESS
PENANCE
CONTRITE
EXAMINE
PROMISE

A MATCHING TEST

Match the sentences with the correct words. Write the letters of the matching words on the blanks.

1 The __B__ helps us be like Jesus.
2 __D__ gave the apostles and priests power to forgive sins.
3 __C__ was sorry when he denied that he knew Jesus.
4 __I__ is anything that may lead us to sin.
5 Sorrow for sins is called __H__.
6 Telling our sins to the priest is called __A__.
7 Choosing to think, say, or do what is wrong or failing to do what we should is a __F__.
8 __J__ said, "Since the Spirit has given us life, let us be led by Him."
9 Jesus gives us __G__ in the Sacrament of Reconciliation.
10 Our __E__ helps us decide what is right or wrong.

A confession
B Holy Spirit
C Peter
D Jesus
E conscience
F sin
G peace
H contrition
I temptation
J Paul

11 GOD'S FAMILY CELEBRATES THE HOLY EUCHARIST

Families share meals together. God's family shares a special meal together. The Eucharistic Celebration or Mass is the special family meal of God's children. Catholics celebrate Sunday by taking part in Mass.

Jesus celebrated the first Mass when He had a special meal with His friends before He died. At Jesus' Last Supper, He took bread and said:
"Take this, all of you, and eat it: this is My Body which will be given up for you."

from Eucharistic Prayer 1

Then Jesus took the cup filled with wine. He thanked His Father, gave the apostles the cup, and said:
"Take this, all of you, and drink from it:
this is the cup of my blood.
It will be shed for you and for all so that sins may be forgiven."

from Eucharistic Prayer 1

Jesus had changed the bread and wine into His Body and Blood. Then He shared Himself as food and drink with His apostles. He told the apostles: "Do this in memory of me."

With these words, Jesus gave His apostles and all priests the power to change bread and wine into His Body and Blood. When Jesus becomes present in the bread and wine, we can share in His death and resurrection.

At every celebration of Mass, Jesus shows His great love.

He offers Himself to God the Father for us.

He teaches us through the readings.

He makes us one with Him and one with God's family in Holy Communion.

He helps us become more like Him so that we can continue His work.

Jesus Gives Us His Blessing

Jesus stays with us in our churches. We can visit Him and speak with Him when we wish.
At special times the priest will give us the blessing of Jesus.
We call this blessing "Benediction." We bless ourselves by making the Sign of the Cross.

WORD BANK
one another
Mass
blessing
Holy Communion

Complete the sentences. Use the WORD BANK.

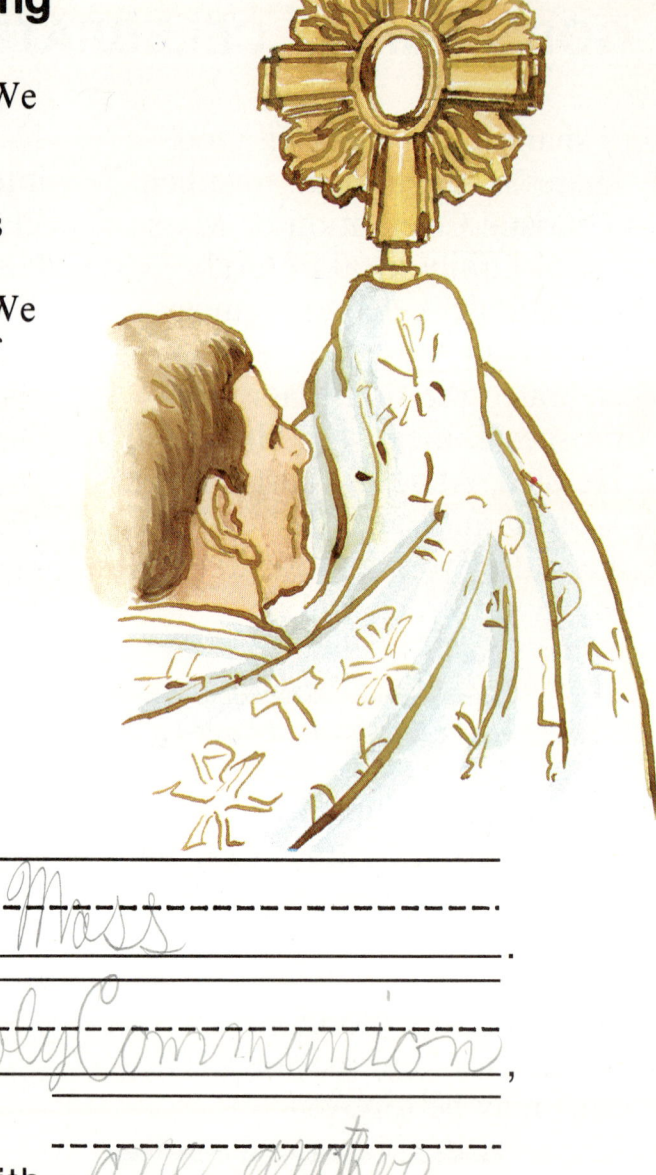

We offer ourselves with Jesus at _Mass_.

When we receive Jesus in _Holy Communion_,

we become one with Him and with _one another_.

We visit Jesus in church and receive His _blessing_.

WE REMEMBER

Why did Jesus give us His Body and Blood in the Eucharist?
Jesus gave us His Body and Blood in the Eucharist so that we can join our offering to His sacrifice to the Father and so that He is with us as our spiritual food.
What is Benediction?
Benediction is a special prayer service to honor Jesus present in the Holy Eucharist and to receive His blessing.

WE RESPOND

I will celebrate your love forever.

Psalm 89:1

Jesus Gives Us His Peace at Mass

Jesus said: My peace I give to you. *Adapted from John 14:27*

PEACE PLEDGE

I will *share* food with those who are hungry.

I will *forgive* those who hurt me.

I will bring *joy* to those who are sad.

I will *help* those in need.

Find the missing words in the PEACE BOX. Write them on the lines.

PEACE BOX
- help
- share
- forgive
- joy

We become more like Jesus in Holy Communion.
We can help carry on His work.
We share His peace by loving others.

Jesus Speaks to Us at Mass

When Jesus lived on earth, He taught the people about His Father's love and the good news of salvation. One day a great number of people followed Jesus to hear what He would say. When Jesus saw the crowd, He went up on a mountainside and sat down.

From there He taught the people and they listened well. But Jesus wanted them to put His words into practice, too. So He told them this story about two men who built houses:

The first man built a beautiful house on rock. When the storms came, the rain poured down and the winds blew hard against it. No harm was done to the house because it was built on rock. It was firm and strong. How wise the first man was to build his house on rock! The second man also built a beautiful house, but he built it on sand. One day the storms came. The rain poured down and the winds blew. It was too much for his house because it was built on sand. It fell and was completely ruined. How foolish the second man was to build his house on sand! Jesus explained the story: "Those who hear my words and follow them are like the wise man who built on rock. Those who hear My words and do not follow them are like the foolish man who built his house on sand."

Adapted from Matthew 7:24-27

When God's family comes together to celebrate Eucharist, Jesus is present. He is present in the priest and in His people. He is present in His Word and in the Eucharist.

The Mass has two main parts: the LITURGY OF THE WORD and the LITURGY OF THE EUCHARIST.

The *Liturgy of the Word* is the celebration of God's speaking to us. God Himself teaches us through His words in the Bible.

A lector (reader) reads the first reading. We listen and say, "Thanks be to God." Then we sing or say a prayer from the psalms.

We stand and sing, "Alleluia, Alleluia, Alleluia!" to welcome the Gospel. To show Jesus speaks to us, we say, "Glory to You, Lord," making a cross on our forehead, our lips, and our heart. We listen with our minds and hearts as the priest or deacon reads from the Gospel of Matthew, Mark, Luke, or John.

Then we say, "Praise to You, Lord Jesus Christ." A priest or deacon explains God's words to us in the homily. When we keep God's words in our hearts, we are like the wise man who built his house on rock.

12 THE EUCHARIST IS A GIFT

We give gifts to show love. Our gifts speak. They say, "See, I love you!" The giver is loved more than the gift. Gifts help us grow in love, too. We love more after we have given or received a gift. God gives gifts to show us love. He has given us the beautiful world and all that is in it. We take His gifts of wheat and grapes and through our work change them into bread and wine. Then at Mass we bring these as gifts to God. God's family gives God what we are and what we have made.

We Offer Our Gifts with Jesus

God gives gifts to us at Mass, too. In the LITURGY OF THE WORD, He gives us the gift of His Word. He tells us how much He loves us and how to live as His loving children. In the LITURGY OF THE EUCHARIST He gives us the gift of Holy Communion.

Jesus gave Himself as a perfect gift to His Father. He did everything to please Him. He died on the cross to save us from sin. Jesus offers the gift of His sacrifice on the cross for all people at every Mass.

The LITURGY OF THE EUCHARIST is like a very special gift exchange. The priest takes our gifts of bread and wine and offers them to God. They are holy gifts because during the Mass the bread and wine become Jesus. Then with Jesus, we offer Jesus and ourselves to God the Father. We do this in the Eucharistic Prayer especially when the priest says:

"Through Him, with Him, in Him, in the unity of the Holy Spirit, all honor and glory is Yours, almighty Father, forever and ever."

We respond to this prayer by saying "Amen" with great joy.

Then God lets us share in this wonderful gift of Jesus. He gives us Jesus in Holy Communion as a gift of His love.

On each line print the letter of the correct answer from the WORD BANK.

WORD BANK
A   God the Father
B   Jesus
C   His Words
D   ourselves
E   love

1   What do all gifts show? ___E___
2   To whom do we offer gifts at Mass? ___A___
3   What do our gifts of bread and wine become during Mass? ___B___
4   To Whom did Jesus give the gift of Himself when He died on the cross? ___A___
5   At Mass what two gifts do we offer to God with Jesus? ___D___ ___B___
6   What gift do we receive from God in the *Liturgy of the Word*? ___C___
7   What gift do we receive in the *Liturgy of the Eucharist*? ___B___

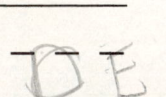

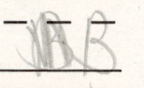

At Mass, we remember the dying and rising of Jesus. We offer ourselves with Jesus to God. We bring our prayers. We bring our joys and our sufferings. We bring all the good things we have done.

Jesus Makes Us One in Him

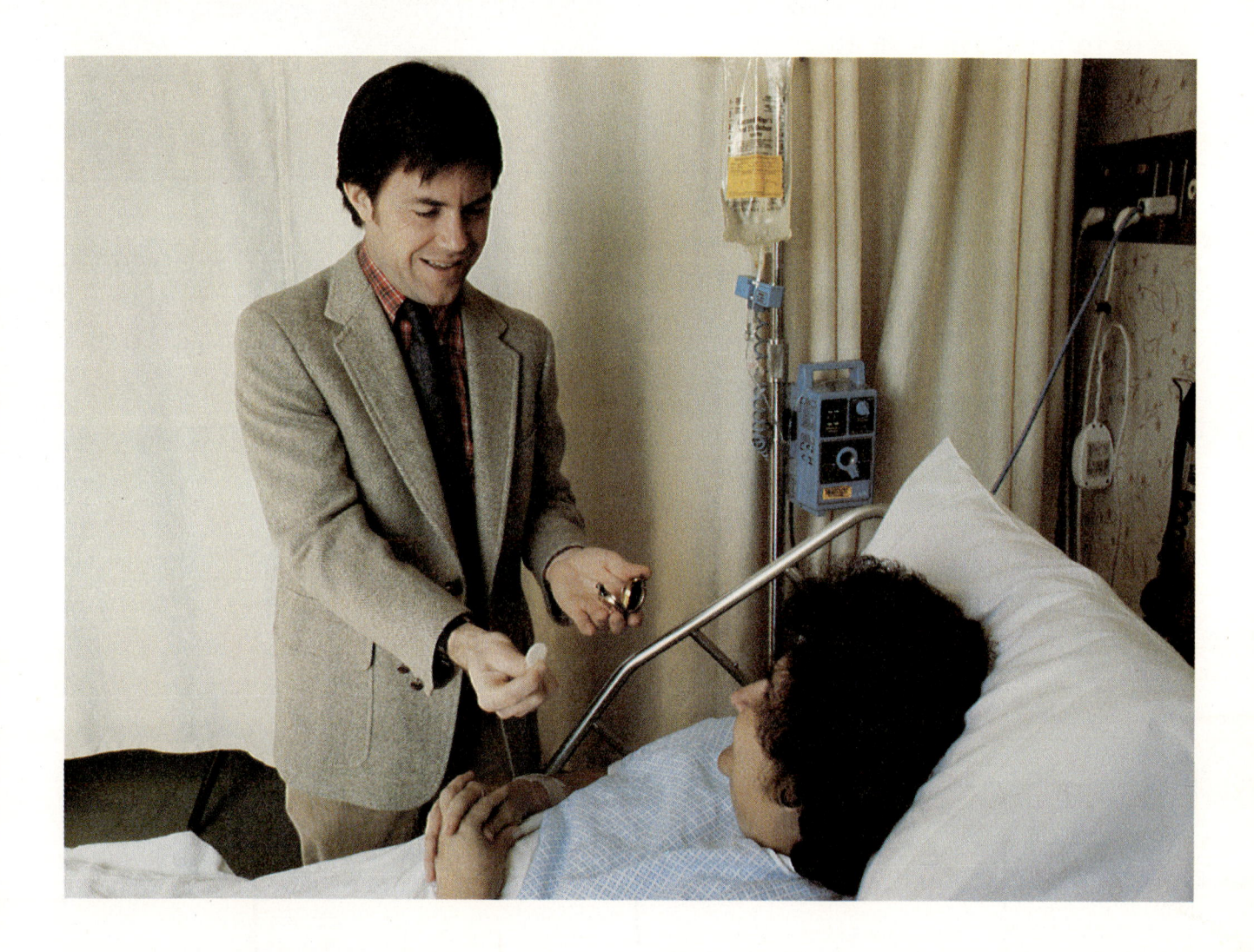

When Jesus gives Himself to us as food and drink in the Holy Eucharist, we become one with Him and His family the Church. We are united with the Father and the Holy Spirit. We are united with Mary and all the angels and saints in heaven. We are united with everyone who shares the Eucharist on earth.

In a letter, St. Paul reminds us that Jesus makes us one in Holy Communion. He said:

"Though we are many, we are one body because we all share in the one bread which is Jesus."

Adapted from 1 Corinthians 10:17

In Holy Communion we come alive with the glorious life of Jesus. We become more like Him. With His grace we can become better persons so that each time we take part in Mass we can offer God a better gift.

During Mass we offered ourselves to God. He accepted us as gift. He filled us with His life and love. Now He can use us to bring His love and care to others. At the end of Mass the priest or deacon tells us, "Go in peace to love and serve the Lord."

Draw a picture in each room of the house to show how you can serve the Lord by bringing His peace and love to others.

WE REMEMBER

What gifts do we offer God at the Eucharistic Celebration?
At the Eucharistic Celebration, with Jesus, we offer Jesus and ourselves to God.

WE RESPOND

May the Lord accept this sacrifice at your hands for the praise and glory of his name for our good and the good of all his church.

from the Ordinary of the Mass

Check the family page for *Theme 12* on page 41.

70

Unit 3 We Keep God's Laws of Love

The Message of the Unit

Love is the supreme commandment. God gave us the Ten Commandments to help us love Him, our neighbor, and ourselves. The children study the commandments, and learn to value and appreciate them as guides to their heavenly home. They are motivated to respond with generosity to God's love by putting God's will first in their lives, and are guided in applying the commandments to daily living. The example of the saints challenges them to keep God's laws with love and courage, trusting in His help and in His promise of eternal happiness.

Sharing the Message as a Family

Family Pages for Themes in Unit 3

A mark in the box indicates that the theme has been presented in class.

Theme 13: ☐   We Learn about the Laws of God, *pages* 78-82

In the Old Testament, God gave the commandments as a pattern for living. In the New Testament, Jesus does not change these laws when He says, "Love God above all things" and "Love your neighbor as yourself." The unique thing Jesus does is to elevate these laws and unify them in Himself; Jesus is the living example of love of God and neighbor.

READ Deuteronomy 5:1-22

DISCUSS
- When God gave the commandments to Moses, how did He show that His law was very important?
- What are the Ten Commandments? (See perform-a-text page 81.)
- Which commandments govern our love for God?
- Which commandments tell us how to love our neighbor and ourselves?

DO
- Have family members re-write the commandments in a positive way. For example: 1. Adore God alone. 2. Honor His name.
- Using hangers, cardboard, and string, make two mobiles of the commandments, one for the first three and another for the last seven. On one side of the card print the number of the commandment; on the opposite side, paste or draw a picture that shows how the commandment can be kept. Label the first mobile *LOVE OF GOD*, the second *LOVE OF OTHERS*. (You may want to label and arrange each card as the commandment is studied.)

PRAY
Thank God often for His commandments by saying: WE LOVE YOUR LAWS, O LORD.

Theme 14: ☐   We Show Our Love for God, *pages* 83-88

God loves each of us with the love of a father. Because we at times allow "other gods" to enter into our lives—persons, places, or things that claim first attention—God commands us to recognize that He is the one true God and to that we must worship Him accordingly. Our worship is expressed through faith, hope, love, prayer, and sacrifice.

READ Exodus 20:1-6

DISCUSS
- Why does God want us to worship Him alone?
- What does He promise to those who keep His commandments?
- What are some of the "other gods" that might lead us away from the true God?
- How can we give first place to God in our lives?

DO
- Review the four kinds of prayer—Adoration, Contrition (prayer expressing sorrow), Thanksgiving, and Supplication (prayer of request). Have different family members make up short examples of each.
- Plan a time for a family "cookie-bake." Make cookies in the shape of the symbols for faith (cross), hope (anchor), love (heart). Decorate them if desired. Remind family members to ask God to fill them with the virtues these cookies represent.

PRAY
When tempted to let other things take God's place in your life, pray:
MY GOD, I LOVE YOU ABOVE ALL THINGS.

Theme 15: ☐ We Love All That Is Holy, *pages* 89-92

God tells us in His second commandment not to misuse His name, and so implies that we should use it properly and with reverence. People who seek to honor God will show reverence for His name and respect the persons, places, and things that are related to the worship of God.

DISCUSS
- What are some examples of misusing God's name in daily life?
- In what other ways can we handle situations which might cause us to use God's name without reverence?
- When is it right or proper to use God's name?
- Besides God's name, what other things related to Him should we respect?

READ Exodus 20:7

PRAY
To show respect for God's name and to make up for those who misuse it, say often:
BLESSED BE GOD. BLESSED BE HIS HOLY NAME.

DO
- Have family members list the names of all the holy persons, places, and things they can think of in three minutes, then compare to see who has the longest list.
- What holy things do you have in your home? How do you show respect for them?
- Look at a map and see how many places you can find that are named after our Lord, the Blessed Mother, the angels, or the saints.
- Sing "Holy God, We Praise Thy Name" or another song that praises God's name.

Theme 16: ☐ We Keep the Lord's Day Holy, *pages* 93-97

For Christians the Lord's Day is Sunday, the day on which we commemorate Christ's resurrection. Thanking God for all His gifts, celebrating Holy Mass with others in the Christian community, and enjoying a day of rest and recreation should be the order of the day. Living Sundays as God wishes will transform our lives.

DISCUSS
- Why did God command us to keep the seventh day holy?
- What day do we Christians keep holy? Why?
- In what ways do we keep Sunday, the Lord's Day, holy?
- What other days does the Church ask us to keep holy in a special way?

READ Exodus 20:8-11

DO
- As a family, plan something you can do to make Sunday a holier and happier day.
- Memorize the Holy Days of Obligation and the date each is celebrated. Quiz each other: For example, "What holy day is celebrated November 1?"
- If there is an older or sickly person living nearby who has to depend on others to get to Mass, offer to take that person to Mass this Sunday or when needed.
- Listen carefully to the homily on Sunday. Set aside a time for the family to share thoughts and ideas about it.

PRAY As a reminder to keep the Lord's Day holy, say often, especially on Sunday:
HOLY IS YOUR DAY, O LORD!

Theme 17: ☐ We Honor and Obey, *pages* 98-101

In giving us the fourth commandment, God shows His love for the family and protects the relationship between parents and children. This commandment also requires us to respect and obey all lawful authority in society and in the Church. We look to the Holy Family as the ideal of family life.

DISCUSS

- What does God command in the fourth commandment?
- What is God's promise to those who keep the fourth commandment?
- How is each family member bound by this commandment?
- Who are some of the other people whom we must respect and obey?

READ Deuteronomy 5:16

DO

- Use family pictures or albums to learn more about your family's history.
- If possible, try to trace back your family tree to some member's first arrival in this country. As an activity for a "Family Night," you might create a family tree starting with that relative. Your tree can be any shape, size, or color.
- Share an experience that made you happy to be a member of your family.
- Each family member may draw the name of another from a bowl or box containing paper slips. He or she may then do something nice for that person during the week.

PRAY To receive the blessing of the Holy Family on your family, say often:
JESUS, MARY, JOSEPH.

Theme 18: ☐ We Respect the Gift of Life, *pages* 102-106

God is the Giver of Life: He sustains it and has absolute power over it. In the fifth commandment, He forbids any thought, word, or act that could in any way harm or endanger ourselves or others. We show appreciation for God's wonderful gift of life by taking care of it and by showing concern and kindness for others.

DISCUSS

- What command did God give to protect the human life He created?
- How do we take care of the gift of life God gave us?
- In what ways can we help others to care for their lives and health?
- How can we best help someone who is sickly or handicapped?

READ Exodus 20:13

DO

- Discuss how good grooming, proper exercise, and healthy eating habits can help keep our bodies in good condition.
- Have different family members tell how the following actions can endanger their lives or the lives of others: not keeping traffic rules; taking drugs; drinking too much; eating junk foods regularly; taking foolish dares.
- Check the daily paper for a story about someone who saved a life or helped another person in danger. Read the story and discuss it. Try to think of other ways of helping people in need.
- Send a card or pay a visit to a friend in the hospital or nursing home; to a shut-in neighbor or parishioner.

PRAY

Show you are grateful to God for the gift of life by saying often:
THANK YOU, LORD, FOR GIVING ME LIFE!

Theme 19: ☐ **Jesus Showed Love and Concern for Others,** *pages* 107-110

The Gospel shows Jesus constantly doing good: meeting the needs of the physically ill by curing them, responding to the spiritually ill by forgiving their sins, fulfilling the needs of all by teaching them how to live more fully in His love. Today, we who are His followers share His love and concern for people, especially for those who are helpless or handicapped.

DISCUSS

- How did the friends of the sick man show that they believed Jesus could cure him?
- Why did Jesus forgive the man's sins before curing him?
- How did Jesus cure the man?
- What was the reaction of the crowd?

READ Mark 2: 1-12

DO

- Play "Round Robin." In the first round, each family member tells two ways he or she helps at home, trying not to repeat what others have said. In the second round, each tells two ways in which he or she is helped by others at home. (Adapt this activity to your own family situation.)
- Sometimes family members can make one another angry or upset. Discuss ways of handling such situations: how to control anger, how to forgive. Talk about similar problems in relationships outside the home.
- Plan a "Family Help" activity. Welcome a new neighbor with a small gift or an offer to help; take a plant cutting to a sick friend or neighbor; decide to help elderly neighbors with such jobs as mowing their lawns or shoveling snow.

PRAY

As a reminder to show love and concern for others, say often:
JESUS, MY BROTHER, HELP ME LOVE YOU IN OTHERS.

Theme 20: ☐ **We Are Faithful to Ourselves and Others,** *pages* 111-116

By creating us in His image and likeness, God endowed us with a special dignity. This dignity is reflected when we respect ourselves and others, when we are faithful in our relationships with others, and when married people are true to their marriage promises.

DISCUSS

- Why are our bodies holy?
- When did the Holy Spirit come to live within us?
- How have we been "bought and paid for"?
- In what ways can we use our bodies for the glory of God?

READ 1 Corinthians 6:19-20

DO

- Many TV programs show neither proper respect for human dignity nor reverence for the human body. What can your family do to show disapproval of such programs?
- Our bodies are "temples of the Holy Spirit." How can family members show that they believe this?
- Discuss how family members can be true to each other and to friends. Why is it important to choose good friends?

PRAY

To help you remember to be faithful to yourself and to others, say:
JESUS, HELP ME TO BE TRUE TO MYSELF, OTHERS, AND YOU!

Theme 21: ☐   **We Respect What God Has Given to Us and to Others,** *pages* **117-119**

God gave us the seventh and tenth commandments to insure the right that every person has to own property, to receive compensation for work done, and to share in the natural resources of the earth. These commandments provide for mutual respect of property. We should try to be satisfied with what we have, and use material things in a responsible way.

DISCUSS

- Why did God command us not to steal?
- What does it mean to "covet" something your neighbor has?
- How can we show God that we appreciate the things He has given us?
- In what ways can we show respect for the property of others?

READ Exodus 20: 15, 17

DO

- List ways in which family members can show respect for things they own or frequently use. (Examples: clothing, books, toys, tools, furniture.)
- How can the family save more electricity, heat, water, and food?
- Discuss how family members show or fail to show respect for one another's personal things. What suggestions for improvement can each member make?
- Plan a "Care and Share" campaign. Give each member of the family a bag or box in which to put things that might be useful to a needy person. These items could then be donated to the St. Vincent de Paul Society, Goodwill Industries, the Salvation Army, or—if it is possible for you to do it directly—to a poor family you may know.

PRAY

To remind ourselves of the gifts of God and how we should care for them, we will say:
THANK YOU, JESUS, FOR ALL YOUR GIFTS.
HELP US TO USE THEM WITH CARE, AND TO LOVINGLY SHARE!

Theme 22: ☐   **We Respect the Gifts of the Earth,** *pages* **120-123**

God created the earth and everything in it to be shared by all people in justice and charity. He expects us to use the gifts of the earth wisely and responsibly.

DISCUSS

- What would happen if there were no plants on earth?
- How do plants and animals help us?
- What other things around, on, and in the earth did God make for our use?
- If God looked on His creation as being "very good," how does He expect us to treat His gifts?

READ Genesis 1: 28-31

DO

- In two minutes, name as many as possible of the natural gifts God has created.
- Discuss what is meant by using these gifts "wisely and responsibly."
- Have a family "Clean Up-Paint Up-Fix Up" week to restore old or damaged things.
- Find out where the nearest recycling center is. Decide what things the family will save and where they will be kept until taken to the center.
- As the weather warms, set aside a week-end afternoon to clean up the yard, trim away dead branches, plant a vegetable and/or flower garden, and to do whatever needs to be done in order to get your small area of "natural resource" into good shape.

PRAY   When you see or use God's gifts of creation, thank Him by saying:
GLORY FOREVER TO GOD! MAY HE FIND JOY IN WHAT HE CREATED!

Adapted from Psalm 104:31

Theme 23: ☐ **We Speak the Truth with Love,** *pages* **124-129**

God is always faithful to His promises: He is the God of Truth. In the eighth commandment, He commands us to speak the truth in all things and to keep our promises. Christ came to earth to "bear witness to the truth"—and He is our "Way" to the Father.

READ
Zechariah 8:16-17

DISCUSS

- In the reading cited above, God speaks to us through the prophet Zechariah. What does He tell us to do?
- What things does God say He hates? Why?
- How can we judge others in a way that leads to peace?
- How is keeping a promise a way of speaking the truth?

DO

- Discuss the importance of telling the truth at home, in school, on the job, and elsewhere. Note how a person who lies is usually punished—people don't believe that person anymore.
- Think of examples of people who had the courage to tell the truth, even when it was hard to do so. (Famous people like Abraham Lincoln; saints like Dominic Savio; current examples.) Share stories about these people with the family.
- Read *Sam, Bangs and Moonshine* by Evaline Ness. Discuss the problems caused by Sam's untruthfulness: her own unhappiness and the danger to a friend. How were the problems solved?
- King Arthur's Knights of the Round Table lived by a special motto: "Live pure, speak true, right wrong, follow the King!" Discuss the value of such a motto. Could it still be used today?

PRAY

When tempted to be untruthful or to neglect keeping a promise, pray:
JESUS, THE WAY, THE TRUTH, THE LIFE,
SHOW ME THE WAY TO BE TRUTHFUL ALWAYS.

Theme 24: ☐ **We Keep God's Laws of Love,** *pages* **130-132**

The Ten Commandments protect our rights and govern our duties to God, others, ourselves, and nature. To those who keep His laws, God promises not only His blessing on earth, but eternal life hereafter.

READ
Psalm 15

DISCUSS

- What does the psalmist mean by "the right to enter God's tent" and "to live on God's holy mountain"?
- Who has the right to do this? Many good acts are listed in this psalm. To which commandment does each refer?
- Why is it hard to do all these things? Whose help can we count on?

DO

- If the family has not made mobiles of the commandments as suggested on the family page for Theme 13, page 72, now would be a good time to do so as a review.
- Quiz each other on the "do" and "don't" aspect of each commandment. The quiz may proceed as follows: one person calls a name and gives a number. The person called recites that commandment and tells what it commands or forbids.
- Using pictures from old magazines or newspapers, make a collage showing how the commandments help us to live good Christian lives.
- "Without laws there would be no life." Do you agree or disagree? Give reasons for your answers.

PRAY

In appreciation for the Ten Commandments and all they do for us, say:
YOUR LAWS, O LORD, BRING JOY TO MY HEART!

13 WE LEARN ABOUT THE LAWS OF GOD

God Gave Us Laws for Living

Narrator: One night Jerry dreamed that he was an astronaut. The head of NASA liked Jerry a great deal and gave him a gift to take along on his first trip to the moon. It was entitled *How to Live on the Moon.*

Head of NASA: Jerry, if you learn the rules in this book and follow them, you will be able to live well on the moon. You will carry out your mission and return safely to earth. Here at Mission Control, we will help you all we can, but you must do your part. Follow the directions in this book, and all will be A-OK.

Jerry: Thank you, sir. I will do everything it says.

Narrator: Then Jerry got into his spaceship and waited for the countdown.

All: TEN, NINE, EIGHT, SEVEN, SIX, FIVE, FOUR, THREE, TWO, ONE. IGNITION. BLAST-OFF!

Narrator: The terrific noise of the blast-off woke Jerry, and he found that he had only been dreaming.

Complete the sentences by choosing the correct words from the WORD BANK.

WORD BANK
stone people
obey   happy
Ten   commands

1 God gave the __Ten__ Commandments to Moses many years ago.

2 God told him to tell the people they must __obey__ them if they wanted to be His __people__.

3 Moses told the people all that the Lord had said. They were __happy__ to hear God's laws and said "We will keep all the __commands__ the Lord has given us."

4 Later God wrote these commands on __stone__ tablets.

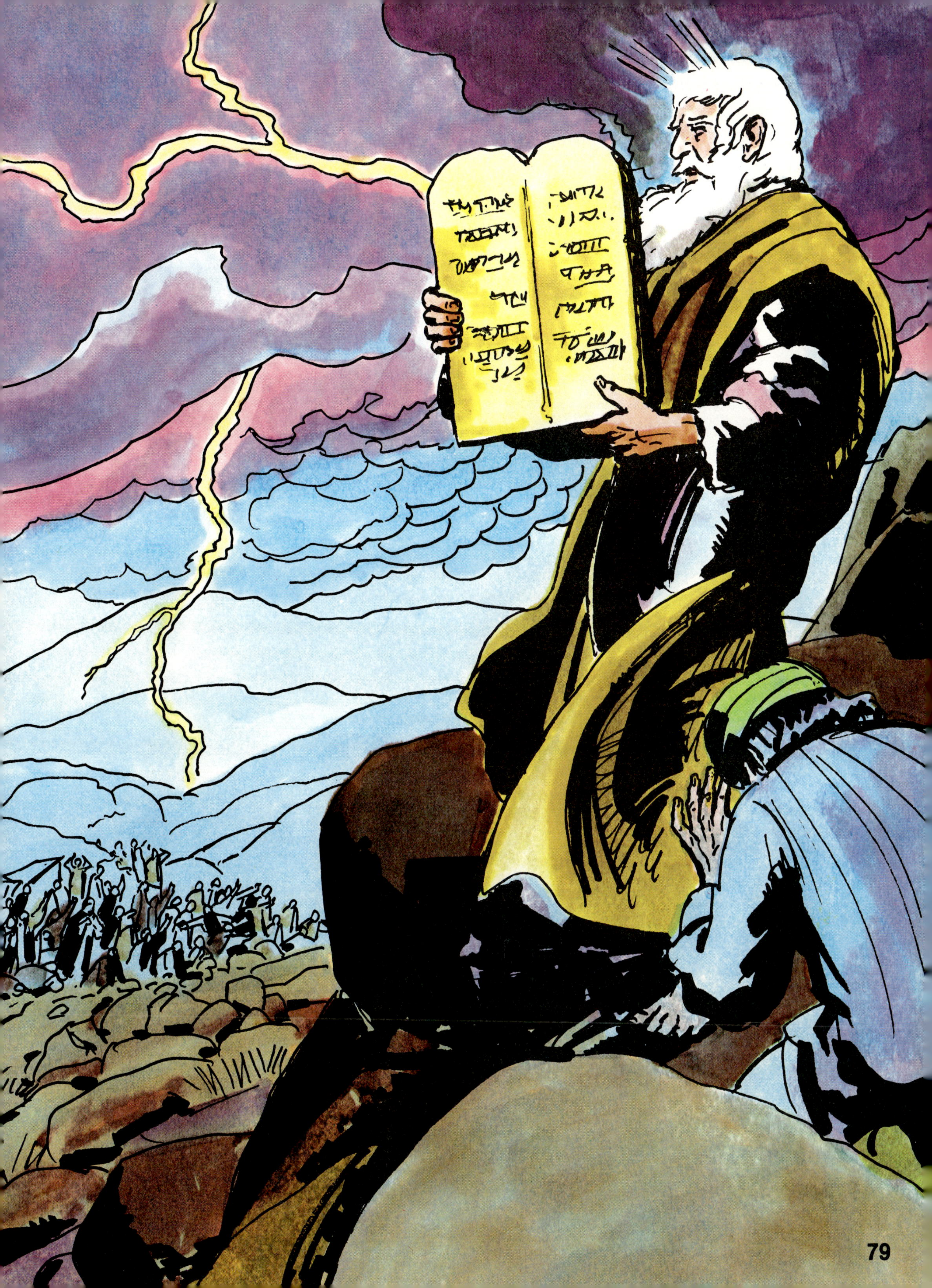

The Commandments Are Laws of Love

God gave us His laws with love.
They show us how to love God and others.
They help us to be happy on earth.
They help us live so that we can be happy with God forever in heaven. There we will be with Mary, the angels, saints, and people we love.

Use the code to find another name for the Ten Commandments. Print the code letter under each number in the heart.

$\underset{4}{L} \underset{1}{A} \underset{8}{W} \underset{6}{S}$
$\underset{5}{O} \underset{3}{F}$
$\underset{4}{L} \underset{5}{O} \underset{7}{V} \underset{2}{E}$

1	2	3	4	5	6	7	8
A	E	F	L	O	S	V	W

Finish writing the Ten Commandments on these stone tablets. The missing words are started for you and can be found in the WORD BANK.

WORD BANK

~~name~~   ~~steal~~   ~~father~~
~~wife~~   ~~kill~~   ~~adultery~~
~~holy~~   ~~gods~~
~~covet~~ ~~false~~

LOVE GOD

1. I, the Lord, am your God. You shall not have other g__ods__ besides Me.

2. You shall not take the n__ame__ of the Lord, your God, in vain.

3. Remember to keep h__oly__ the Sabbath day.

LOVE OTHERS

4. Honor your f__ather__ and your mother.

5. You shall not k__ill__.

6. You shall not commit a__dultery__.

7. You shall not s__teal__.

8. You shall not bear f__alse__ witness against your neighbor.

9. You shall not covet your neighbor's w__ife__.

10. You shall not c__ovet__ anything that belongs to your neighbor.

WE REMEMBER

Why did God give us the Ten Commandments?

God gave us the Ten Commandments to help us to be happy and holy on earth and to be happy with Him forever in heaven.

WE RESPOND

I will keep all the commands that the Lord has given me.

Adapted from Exodus 24:3

God's People Love His Commandments

Here is one of the psalms
that God's people say:

How can a person be good and happy?

By obeying Your commands.

With all my heart I try to keep them.

Help me to obey Your Laws.

I love Your promise with all my heart.

It helps me to do what pleases You.

I praise You, O Lord;

Teach me Your commandments.

Then with my lips I will repeat

The words of Your commands.

I rejoice because I have Your laws.

They are better than great riches.

I will think of Your teachings

And study Your ways.

I find my joy in Your Laws.

I remember Your words.

Adapted from Psalm 119:9-16

Your Word, O Lord, is the joy of my heart. I sing Your prais-es by night and by day, and walk with glad-ness a - long Your way.

14 WE SHOW OUR LOVE FOR GOD

God Gives Us Gifts

God our Father made us and gives us life. He gives us all the beautiful things in the world. Everything we have is a gift from Him.

God wants us to love His gifts because he made them and they are good. They show us His glory and tell us of His love. God's gifts lead us to worship Him.

We praise You, O Lord, for all Your gifts are wonderful!

Adapted from Psalm 145:4-5

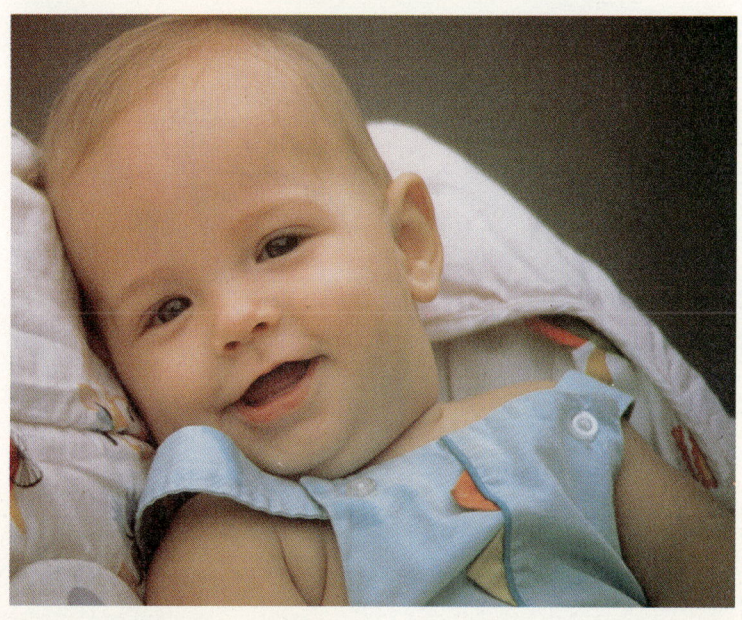

God Asks for Our Love

God is good and much greater than all His gifts. He wants us to love Him above everything else. He knows all things and tells us what is true. He wants us to believe in Him. As our loving Father, He always cares for us. He wants us to hope in Him.

In His first commandment God says, "I, the Lord, am your God. You shall not have other gods besides Me."

He says, "Give Me your love."

Jesus is God's best gift to us. He shows us how to love God our Father above everything else. He shows us how to adore God. He teaches us how to pray.

Use the WORD BANK to find the word that completes each sentence. The first letter of each word is given for you.

God's gifts show us His g__oodness__.

God calls us to a__dore__ Him.
God tells us what is true.

He wants us to b__elieve__ in Him.
God cares for us.

He wants us to h__ope__ in Him.

God wants us to l__ove__ Him more than His gifts. We show our love when we p__ray__ to Him.

WORD BANK
love
goodness
pray
believe
hope
adore

84

We Give God Our Love in Prayer

When we pray, we lift up our minds and hearts to God. We think of Him and love Him. God listens to us and speaks to us, too. He loves us.

Jesus showed us how to pray. He taught us how to pray in the Our Father.

When we pray we love, praise, and thank God. We tell Him we are sorry and ask Him to give us all we need. A long time ago, God's people prayed like this when they said the psalms.

WE REMEMBER

What is the first commandment?
The first commandment is:
"I, the Lord, am your God. You shall not have other gods besides me."

WE RESPOND

I will pray every day.

Check the family page for *Theme 14* on page 72.

We Pray the Psalms

1 A PSALM OF ~~sorrow~~ *thanks*

I give thanks

to the Lord,

for He is good.

His love is everlasting!

Adapted from Psalm 118:1

2 A PSALM OF *praise*

Let all the earth cry out

to God with joy.

Sing praise to the

glory of His name.

Adapted from Psalm 66:1-2

3 A PSALM OF *sorrow*

Lord, forgive

the wrong I have

done.

I confess

my sin to You.

Adapted from Psalm 32:5

4 A PSALM OF _petition_

Lord, come

to my help.

I waited

for the Lord

and He stooped

down to help me.

Adapted from Psalm 40:1

5 A PSALM OF _love_

I love You,

Lord.

You take care

of me.

Adapted from Psalm 18:1

Here are some psalms. The WORD BANK will help you find the word that tells the kind of prayer each one is, Print the word that belongs on each blank.

WORD BANK

~~Sorrow~~   ~~Petition~~   Praise
~~Love~~   Thanks

We Honor Mary, the Angels, and the Saints in Prayer

God wants us to love and honor those who live in heaven with Him. Mary, Jesus' mother and ours, lives there. Heaven is home for the angels who bring us God's messages. God's special friends and ours, the saints, live there, too. They pray for us and ask God to bless us. One day we will live with them in heaven.

We show our love for Mary, the angels, and the saints by praying to them and by imitating them. When we honor them, we honor God, Who made them.

Read the clues and fill in the puzzle.

Puzzle answers filled in:
- 1 Across: MARY
- 2 Down: ANGEL
- 3 Across: SAINTS

Across:
1 She is our Blessed Mother.
3 They are God's special friends and ours.

Down:
2 They bring God's messages to us.

WE REMEMBER

What is prayer?
Prayer is lifting up our minds and hearts to God.

WE RESPOND

To You I lift up my soul, O my God.

Adapted from Psalm 25:1

15 WE LOVE ALL THAT IS HOLY

We Praise the Name of the Lord

GOD

We give our love to God when we keep the second commandment which says:
"You shall not take the name of the Lord your God in vain."

Adapted from Exodus 20:7

When Jesus was on earth, He told us to call God our Father and to pray:

HALLOWED BE THY NAME

YAHWEH
LORD
FATHER
JESUS
CHRIST
HOLY
SPIRIT

How great

is Your name,

O Lord,

our God,

through all

the earth!

Adapted from Psalm 8:1

This means that we use God's name in a way that shows love and respect. God's name is holy because He is holy. Each name that we call God tells how good or powerful He is.

89

When we sing and pray we use many of the names of God. Unscramble the letters and write the name of God that belongs on each blank.

SUJES ____JESUS____ means "God saves."

HCRSTI Another name for Jesus is ____CHRIST____.

YHOL TRISPI We honor the Third Person of the Blessed Trinity when we say ____HOLY____ ____SPIRIT____.

DLOR We call God ____LORD____ because He rules over heaven and earth.

HAFTRE Jesus told us to call God our ____FATHER____.

YHWHEA God told Moses that His name is ____YAHWEH____.

We Respect All That Is Holy

One day when Jesus went to the temple, He saw many people buying and selling animals. Other people were walking around and talking. Jesus was angry when He saw that people were not honoring God in that holy place. He knocked over tables which had piles of money on them. He ordered people who were selling things out of the temple.

Then Jesus said, "My Father's house is a house of prayer. You have made it a den of thieves."

Adapted from Matthew 21:12-14

Jesus wanted the people to respect the temple as a holy place. Today, he wants us to respect all holy *persons*, *places*, and *things*. God our Father taught us the same thing in the second commandment. Holy *persons*, *places*, and *things* help us think of God. When we honor what is holy, we praise and honor God.

Certain *places* are called "holy" because they are special places where people pray and worship.

Draw a picture of a holy place.

What are some other holy places?

church

91

All persons are called to holiness. Some are called to give themselves entirely to God and His work.

Draw a picture of some people who do special work for God.

Who are some other holy people?
_____
_____
_____
_____

Choose the holy name of God that you like best. Use that name to tell God that you love Him.
_____
_____

Certain *things* are called "holy" because they remind us of God, or because they are used when we pray.

Draw a picture of some holy things.

What are some other holy things?
_____
_____
_____
_____

WE REMEMBER

What is the second commandment? The second commandment is: "You shall not take the name of the Lord, your God, in vain."

WE RESPOND

I will honor God's name and respect all holy persons, places, and things.

Check the family page for *Theme 15* on page 73.

16 WE KEEP THE LORD'S DAY HOLY

God Tells Us to Keep His Day Holy

When God created the world, He worked for six days and rested on the seventh. He blessed the seventh day and made it holy. In His third commandment God told His people to do as He did. He said, "Remember to keep holy the Sabbath day. You may work for six days, but you must keep the seventh day for the Lord."

Adapted from Exodus 20:8-10

God's people loved Him and remembered what He said. They were very careful to keep the Sabbath day holy. They went to the temple or synagogue to worship together. They rejoiced with others. They rested from work. They did all their work the day before the Sabbath.

The early Christians kept Sunday as the Lord's Day for two reasons. Jesus rose from the dead on Easter Sunday morning, and He sent His Spirit on a Sunday. Christians celebrated Sunday to show they believed in Jesus. They came together for the "breaking of the bread." This means that they celebrated Eucharist or Mass to remember Jesus' dying and rising.

This WORD BANK will help you answer the questions on this page:

Rested	Jesus rose on Easter
Sunday	Sunday
Prayed	Eucharist
Rejoiced	Sabbath

Which day was the Lord's day _____ for God's people? _____

How did God's people keep the Sabbath holy?

1 _____

2 _____

3 _____

Which day did the early Christians keep _____ as the Lord's day? _____

Why did they celebrate on Sunday?

_____

What did they celebrate together?

_____

We Celebrate Sundays and Holy Days

In His third commandment, God tells us that He wants us to keep Sunday holy. The Church tells us to keep this day holy by celebrating Mass and resting from our work. As Catholics we praise and thank God together at the Eucharistic celebration on Saturday evening or Sunday. We celebrate the new life Jesus won by His dying and rising. We make Sunday a day of rest and celebration. We enjoy ourselves and give joy to others. Celebrating each Sunday reminds us of the big celebration we will one day enjoy in heaven.

As Catholic Christians, we come together for Mass on holy days to celebrate special feasts in honor of Jesus, Mary, and the saints.

HOW DO WE MAKE SUNDAY A DAY OF SPECIAL CELEBRATION?

CAN YOU NAME SOME HOLY DAYS THAT WE CELEBRATE IN OUR COUNTRY?

MAKE THE SUN SHINE ON THE LORD'S DAY

On each sunray, print one way in which we can celebrate Sunday.

These words may help you: *Be kind, Rest, Play, Sing, Pray, Celebrate, Dress up, Share.*

Print *Celebrate Eucharist* in the center of the sun.

Check the family page for *Theme 16* on page 73.

WE REMEMBER

What is the third commandment?
The third commandment is: "Remember to keep holy the Sabbath day."

WE RESPOND

I will keep the Lord's Day holy by celebrating Eucharist on Sundays and holy days.

We Love the Lord

MAKE A JIGSAW PUZZLE

Love God's NAME

Directions:
1. Print a motto on the one side of a card and design it.
2. Draw dotted lines on the other side to divide your card into ten pieces.
3. Cut your card on the dotted lines and put the pieces in an envelope.
4. Exchange your envelope with a classmate and work out each other's puzzle.

SOME MOTTOS TO USE:

LOVE GOD WITH ALL YOUR HEART
LIFT UP YOUR HEARTS
TRUST IN THE LORD
PRAY TO THE LORD
LOVE GOD'S NAME
LOVE THE EUCHARIST

WORD BANK
THANKS
SORROW
PETITION
PRAISE

A PRAYER PUZZLE

Besides the prayer of love, there are other kinds of prayers. Use the WORD BANK to find the other kinds of prayers and write their names on the lines.

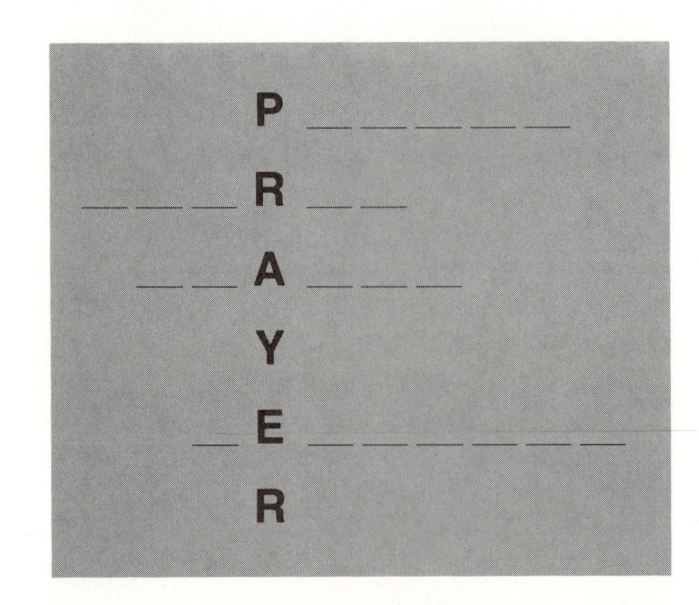

P _ _ _ _ _
_ _ _ _ R _ _ _
_ _ _ A _ _ _ _
_ _ Y _ _
_ E _ _ _ _ _ _
R

GUIDE THE FOOTSTEPS TO THE SENTENCES

Find the words in the footsteps that will complete the sentences below.
Fill in the correct words.

1. God gave us the Ten Commandments to help us reach _____.
2. The first three commandments tell us _____ to love _____.
3. In the first commandment, God said, "I, the _____, am your God."
4. "You shall not have other _____ besides Me."
5. Prayer is the lifting up of our minds and _____ to God.
6. When we honor Mary, the angels, or the _____, we honor God, Who made them.
7. In the second commandment, God tells us not use His name in _____.
8. We respect holy _____, places and things.
9. In the third commandment, God tells us to keep holy the _____ day.
10. Catholic Christians celebrate Eucharist on Saturday evenings or Sundays and on _____.

Footsteps: SABBATH, HEARTS, GOD, HEAVEN, LORD, HOLY DAYS, GODS, SAINTS, VAIN, PERSONS

17 WE HONOR AND OBEY

We Bring Happiness to Our Families

Families are very different in many ways. But they should all be alike in one way. Members of a family should love and care about each other. Children should honor and respect their parents.

Jesus belonged to a family. Mary was His mother and Joseph His foster father. Jesus loved the parents His heavenly Father had given Him. He kept the fourth commandment,

"Honor your father and your mother."

He respected and obeyed them although He was greater than they were because He was God's Son.

God shows us how precious the gift of life is by giving us this commandment. He wants us to honor our mothers and fathers who helped to give us life. He promises special blessings if we do.

God asks our parents to love and care for us. They are to give us what we need to grow as God's children. Our parents make many sacrifices for us. When we honor and respect them, we please God. We bring happiness to our families and to ourselves.

The words on the HAPPINESS WHEEL tell how we honor our parents.
We love, respect, help, and obey them.
We pray for them.

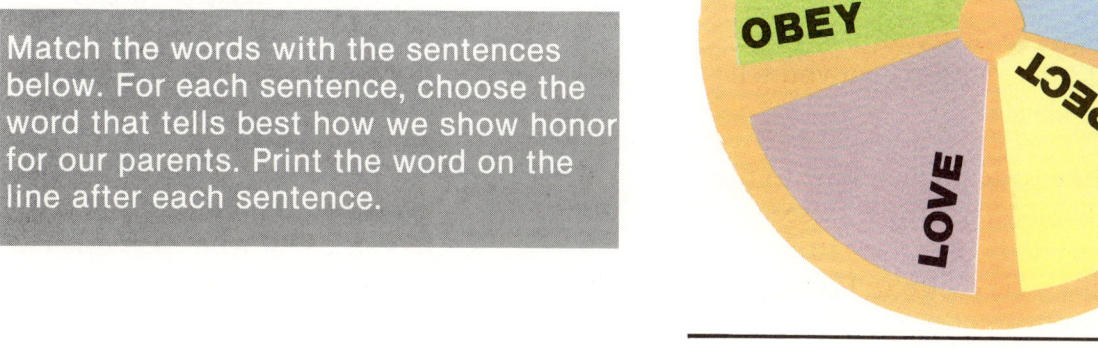

Match the words with the sentences below. For each sentence, choose the word that tells best how we show honor for our parents. Print the word on the line after each sentence.

1   We do what our parents tell us.

2   We talk politely to our parents.

3   We do the dishes.

4   We do kind things for our parents.

5   We listen politely to our parents.

6   We ask God to bless our parents.

7   We carry out the trash.

8   We say nice things about our parents.

9   We clean our rooms and pick up our things.

10 We come when our parents call us.

We Respect and Obey Those Who Guide Us

Teacher: Today we are going to talk about leaders. Has anyone here ever been chosen to be a leader in a game?

Nicky: (Smiling proudly, raises his hand.) Me! I'm always team captain!

Teacher: I can see that you like being a leader, Nicky. Can you tell the class why?

Nicky: I like to tell others how to play a good game. I like to see everybody play hard to win. I like everybody to listen and do as I say.

Teacher: (Laughing.) *I* also like everyone to listen and do as I say! Does that make me a leader, too?

Susan: Yes, but you're not like *him*!

Teacher: Nicky and I guide you in different ways. There are many different leaders who try to guide us to do what is right. Can you think of some others?

Andy: People like the mayor.

Emily: And the pope!

Teacher: That's right, we have leaders in our Church and in our government—and there are even more. All leaders need the help of those they lead in order to do a good job. For instance, what can you do during a game to help Nicky be a good leader?

Mike: Watch for his signals and try to work well with each other as a team.

Andy: Always listen to what Nicky says.

Emily: What if someone who is our captain asks us to cheat to win a game?

Nicky: I would never do that!

Teacher: I know you wouldn't, Nicky. But one thing we must always remember is that we never obey *anyone* who tells us to do something we know is wrong.

FOURTH COMMANDMENT WORD SCRAMBLE

> Unscramble the letters and print the correct word on each line.

1. Which commandment tells us how to honor our fathers and mothers? (ortufh) __fourth__

2. What word means to love, respect, and obey? (nohro) __honor__

3. What does the fourth commandment help us bring to our families? (piespahsn) __happiness__

4. What can we do for parents who are not with their families or who have died? (ypar for them) __pray for them__

5. Who are others besides our parents who guide and protect us? (daeresl) __leaders__

6. We do not obey anyone who tells us to do (rgnow) __wrong__.

7. When we honor our parents, we please (odG) __God__.

WE REMEMBER
What is the fourth commandment?

The fourth commandment is: "Honor your father and your mother."

WE RESPOND
I will love, respect, and obey my parents and others who guide and protect me.

Check the family page for *Theme 17* on page 74.

18 WE RESPECT THE GIFT OF LIFE

Our Life Is Precious

God said,
"Let us make man
in our own image,
in the likeness of ourselves, . . ."

Genesis 1:26

Life Is God's Gift

Life is not a gift we keep
for ourselves.
It always belongs to God.
He created all life out of love.
The life of every person,
even the tiniest baby,
belongs to God.

All life is precious to God.
He wants us to take care
of our own life
and the lives of others.

He wants us to respect life
and protect it.
He tells us this
in the fifth commandment:
"You shall not kill."

Exodus 20:13

How can you tell that the people
in these pictures love life?

God Wants Us to Take Care of Life

Everyone who really loves Jesus is kind to others.

Peter Claver was a Spanish priest. He spent his life helping blacks in the West Indies. Many blacks were brought there to be slaves. Father Claver saw how cruel slavery was. He met the slave ships as they arrived from Africa. The slaves were very hungry. Father Claver gave them fresh fruit. He gave medicine to the sick. He helped the dying.

After Father Claver helped these people, he told them about Jesus. He taught them to offer their sufferings to God and told them that one day they would join God in heaven. Many slaves asked to be baptized. Father Claver baptized more than forty-thousand slaves before he died. Now he is in heaven, and we call him St. Peter Claver.

WE REMEMBER
What is the fifth commandment?
The fifth commandment is: "You shall not kill."

WE RESPOND
I thank God for the gift of life. I will respect life and show kindness toward others.

Check the family page for *Theme 18* on page 75.

Find out what we can call anyone who keeps the fifth commandment. Read the sentences, follow the directions, and put the letters in the LIFE PUZZLE.

1. If you would help someone who was hurt, put "L" in space 1.

2. If you try to eat the right kinds of food to keep healthy, put "I" in space 2.

3. If you take drugs only when a doctor tells you, put "F" in space 3.

4. If you would forgive someone who hurt you, put "E" in spaces 4, 7, 9, and 12.

5. If you try not to say mean things when you feel angry, put "R" in spaces 6, 10, and 13.

6. If you don't fight when someone hurts you, put "P" in space 5.

7. If you try to obey traffic and fire laws, put "S" in space 8.

8. If you would help feed hungry people, put "V" in space 11.

Christians Are Kind and Merciful

A lawyer asked Jesus what to do in order to win eternal life. Jesus told him to love God and his neighbor. Then the lawyer asked Jesus, "Who is my neighbor?" Jesus answered by telling this story:

A man going down the road was attacked by robbers. They took his money and clothes and left him half dead. Soon a man who served God came by. He saw the man but went right on. Another traveler also saw the dying man, but he passed right by. Then a Samaritan came along. He cleaned and bandaged the man's wounds. Then he put the man on his donkey and rode to an inn, where he cared for him. The next day, the Samaritan gave two silver coins to the innkeeper and said, "Take care of this man. If you need more money, I will repay you on my way back."

Jesus then asked, 'Which of these three was a good neighbor to the wounded man?" The lawyer replied, "The man who showed kindness and mercy to him." Jesus said, "Be kind and merciful like him."

Adapted from Luke 10:25-37

HOW ARE THESE PEOPLE LIKE THE GOOD SAMARITAN?

1. Mr. and Mrs. Jones were an elderly couple who lived next door to Peter. One night it snowed very hard. Peter and his friend Tim shoveled their walk. When Mr. Jones offered to reward them, Peter and Tim wouldn't take any money.

2. Mary and Sue met Mrs. Kramer in the store. She was trying to watch her three small children and to shop at the same time. The two girls took care of the children while Mrs. Kramer shopped.

3. Mark's big sister had prepared supper for the family. When Mark sat down to eat, he noticed she had prepared some food he didn't like. Mark ate it without complaining and thanked his sister for the meal.

Work the puzzle on the globe. Use the hints below and the WORD BANK.

Down:
1. The fifth commandment tells us to care for _____.
2. All life belongs to _____.
3. When we forgive others, we show _____.

Across:
4. When we say or do loving things we show _____.

WORD BANK
God
mercy
life
kindness

106

19 JESUS SHOWED LOVE AND CONCERN FOR OTHERS

Kind Words and Actions Bring Joy to Others

Jesus said,
"I have come
that you may have life—
and have it to the full."

Adapted from John 10:10

A man named Jairus rushed through the crowd to reach Jesus. "My daughter has just died," he said. "Come, lay Your hand on her and she will live."

Jesus went with Jairus to his house. He took the little girl by the hand and she got up. Jesus gave life back to her and gave joy to Jairus.

Adapted from Matthew 9:18-19, 23-25

MEET THE NEEDS OF OTHERS

We can't perform miracles to help people, but we can do many thoughtful things for them.

Mark + in Box 1 if you can say a prayer asking God to help.
Mark o in Box 2 if you can think of a sacrifice you could make for others.
Mark ♡ in Box 3 if you can think of something loving to say or do.

1 PRAY

2 SACRIFICE

3 HELP

Be ready to explain each mark that you make.

1 2 3

☐ ☐ ☐ Your mother has a bad headache.

☐ ☐ ☐ Your neighbor's home burned down.

☐ ☐ ☐ A flood destroyed a town.

☐ ☐ ☐ A classmate is sick.

☐ ☐ ☐ Hospitals in India need medicine.

☐ ☐ ☐ Your father lost his job.

☐ ☐ ☐ A new student enters your class.

☐ ☐ ☐ Your friend tried out for a team but didn't make it.

☐ ☐ ☐ Your little brother can't read as well as he should.

Forgiving Love Heals People

One day Jesus was teaching in a house. Many people gathered to hear Him speak. They crowded into the house and around the door.

In the crowd was a paralyzed man who wanted to see Jesus.
Because he couldn't get into the house, his friends carried him to the roof. They lifted up part of the roof until they had a large opening. Then they lowered the sick man on his stretcher.

Jesus stopped teaching. He looked with love at the sick man and said, "My son, your sins are forgiven."

Then He cured the man's body. The man got up, picked up his stretcher, and walked out in front of everyone.

Adapted from Mark 2:1-12

Unscramble these words. They will tell you how your love can "heal" others. The numbers will help you. Print each word under the HOME OF PEACE.

| E A H R S |
| 5 3 2 4 1 |

| L E P H |
| 3 2 4 1 |

| Y A R P |
| 4 3 2 1 |

| V I R G F E O |
| 6 5 3 4 1 7 2 |

WE REMEMBER

What does Jesus say about forgiving others?
Jesus says, "If you forgive others, your heavenly Father will forgive you."

Adapted from Matthew 6:14

HOME OF PEACE

WE RESPOND

I will forgive those who hurt me.

Check the family page for *Theme 19* on page 75.

109

Jesus' Kindness Helped People in Need

Bartimaeus was blind. He sat by the roadside and begged for what he needed.

One day he heard that Jesus was passing by. He called out, "Jesus, Son of David, have pity on me." When some people tried to make him keep quiet, he shouted all the louder. He wanted Jesus to help him. Jesus stopped and asked him, "What do you want me to do for you?" Bartimaeus answered, "Lord, I want to see." Jesus was pleased with the man's faith. He healed Bartimaeus and said, "Go, your faith has saved you."

Adapted from Mark 10:46-52

HOW CAN KINDNESS GIVE A HAPPY ENDING TO THESE STORIES?

1. As Brian was hurrying down the hall, he bumped into a little boy on his way to the lunchroom. The boy's lunchbox opened, spilling his lunch on the floor.

2. All of Ellen's friends brought money to buy a treat, but Ellen wasn't able to bring any.

3. Chris and Mike were good friends. Both boys tried out for a part in a play. Chris got a part but Mike didn't.

4. Sue's brother teased her about her new haircut.

5. Tracey's friend won't talk to her because Tracey went skating with other friends and didn't invite her.

Make up your own story about a boy or girl who needs kindness.

20 WE ARE FAITHFUL TO OURSELVES AND OTHERS

Our Bodies Are Good

Have you ever watched the Olympics? The beauty and grace of the gymnasts, divers, ice skaters and other athletes fill us with delight and awe. They make us realize how wonderful our human bodies are.

God gave us the gift of our bodies when He made us. Scripture tells us,

"God created man in the image of himself, male and female he created them."

Genesis 1:27

We should be proud to be a boy or to be a girl. We should be proud of the wonderful body God has given us and respect it.

Our bodies help us to live and grow as human persons. One of the most important things we do as human persons is to form friendships. We let others know who we are, and we come to know and love them. In all our friendships, God asks us to be true to ourselves and to others. We are true to ourselves when we keep our bodies holy.

We Are True to Ourselves

Long ago St. Paul wrote a letter to some people who had been Christians just a short time. He wanted them to know how holy they were. Now the letter is meant for us. St. Paul tells us how to be true to ourselves.

Dear Friends in Christ,

Keep yourselves holy. Your body is the temple of the Holy Spirit. He has lived within you ever since you were baptized. You do not belong to yourselves but to God. He bought and paid for you. So use your body to give glory to God. May the love of our Lord Jesus Christ be with you.

Paul the Apostle

Adapted from 1 Corinthians 6:19-20

How can we keep ourselves holy? Draw a line to connect the beginning of each sentence with the right ending.

1 Look at
2 Make
3 Pray
4 Receive
5 Respect

- to Mary.
- only good movies, TV shows, books and pictures.
- sacrifices to show love for God and others.
- your body and those of others.
- Holy Communion and the Sacrament of Reconciliation often.

We Are Faithful to Others

Friends are persons who care about each other. They like to be together and to do things together. They help each other in times of need.

Good friends can always count on each other. They are faithful. They help each other to love God and to do what is right.

God wants us to have many good friends. He is pleased when we are true to them.

The sixth and ninth commandments help us to be faithful:

"You shall not commit adultery."

"You shall not covet your neighbor's wife."

Exodus 20:14-17

Sometimes a man and a woman have a special kind of friendship. They want to share their lives and to start a new family. They get married in order to do this. On their wedding day, husbands and wives make special promises to each other before God. They promise to love and care for each other always.

When a man and woman get married, they receive the Sacrament of Marriage. With this sacrament, God helps the husband and wife to keep their promises.

Read the sentences and fill in the missing words. Use the WORD BANK.

WORD BANK
love
promises
care
other
God

On their wedding day, a man and woman make _____ to _____ and to each _____.

They promise to _____ and _____ for each other always.

Draw two wedding rings in the heart to show that a husband and wife promise to love each other always.

WE REMEMBER
What is the sixth commandment? "You shall not commit adultery."

What is the ninth commandment? "You shall not covet your neighbor's wife."

WE RESPOND
I will respect myself and others and be faithful to my friends.

Check the family page for *Theme 20* on page 75.

We Are Temples of the Holy Spirit

WHERE IS GOD PRESENT?

God is present everywhere, but He is present in a special way in the places pictured here. Finish each of the pictures by connecting the numbered dots. On the line under each picture, name what it shows. Use the WORD BANK.

WORD BANK
church
temple
baptized person

115

Micky: Hi, Mom. We're home!

Judy: Hi, Mom. Guess what! I learned something so great today that I'm never going to forget it. It's about something that is like a temple or a church. It belongs to God because He made it. He came to live in it at Baptism. Do you know what it is?

Mom: Your body or the body of anyone who is baptized.

Judy: Right, Mom. Think of it: we're temples of the Holy Spirit.

Micky: Am I a temple, too?

Mom: Yes, Micky. It's so wonderful that I hope you'll always remember it.

Judy: That's just what St. Paul told us to do. Do you know what else he said?

Micky: No. Tell us, Judy.

Judy: He said we should use our bodies to give glory to God. That means we should do good things with our bodies. (Suddenly smiling.) Mom, do you think it would be good for my body if I ate some of your homemade cookies?

Micky: Me, too, Mom!

Mom: (Laughing.) I think it would be good if you both changed your clothes first, washed your hands, and *then* ate some of my cookies.

Judy and Micky: Okay, Mom!

21 WE RESPECT WHAT GOD HAS GIVEN TO US AND TO OTHERS

God Gives Us the Things We Need

God loves the human persons He made. He put into the world everything we need to lead good lives.

All of us have a right to what we need. But God wants us to use His gifts in the right way. We should take care of our things and the things of others. We should share with others.

How can we take care of what we have?

When can we share with others?

We show love for others when we respect what they have. It is wrong to take what belongs to them. In the seventh commandment God says: "You shall not steal."

Exodus 20:15

How do others feel when we respect their things?

If we are living good, healthy lives, we should be satisfied with what we have. God tells us this in the tenth commandment when He says: "You shall not covet anything that belongs to your neighbor."

Adapted from Exodus 20:17

Why should we be satisfied with what we have?

We Respect the Property of Others

Everyone has a right to own things. God wants us to respect other's rights. He wants us to respect other people's things and to be honest and fair in all we do.

We show respect for other people's things by using them in the right way. We should be careful not to damage, ruin, nor lose what belongs to others. If we damage anything, we must repair it or pay for it.

It is wrong to steal from people or to cheat them. A person who takes anything that belongs to someone else must always return it to the owner or pay for it.

We ask others before using their things. We return the things we borrow. When we find things, we try to return them to their owner. When we take tests, we do not cheat. When we play games, we are fair and follow the rules.

Read the sentences and fill in the letters to complete the missing words.

We respect others and share because we c __ r __.

We respect t __ __ g __ that belong to others.

When we take a test, we are h __ n __ __ t; we do not cheat.

We make up to others when we d __ m __ ge their property.

We are satisfied with what we have and th __ __ k God for His gifts.

WE REMEMBER

What is the seventh commandment?
The seventh commandment is: "You shall not steal."

What is the tenth commandment?
The tenth commandment is: "You shall not covet your neighbor's goods."

WE RESPOND

I will be honest and fair.
I will be satisfied with what I have.

Check the family page for *Theme 21* on page 76.

The sentences show children choosing to do right or wrong. Put a ✓ on the blank if the sentence tells about someone who is following either the seventh or tenth commandment. If the sentence shows someone not keeping either of these commandments, write the word from the WORD BOX that tells what is wrong.

WORD BOX
stealing
cheating
envy
damaging property

1 Karen told the librarian that she accidentally tore a page in a book. _____

2 Alex took a toy from the counter in the store and hid it under his coat. _____

3 After accidentally breaking Mr. Duffey's window, some boys offered to pay for it. _____

4 Jonathan cut in front of someone in line so that he could get another turn at bat. _____

5 Joan returned the pencil she borrowed from her classmate. _____

6 Laura was sad because she couldn't have Rita's necklace. _____

7 To get a higher grade, Nicky changed an answer after tests were returned. _____

8 Joe shared the candy his uncle gave him. _____

9 Betty took a notebook from the store without paying for it. _____

10 Carl ran through his neighbor's new garden. _____

22 WE RESPECT THE GIFTS OF THE EARTH

God made all the things on earth.
In the Bible we read:
"God saw all that He had made,
and indeed it was very good. . . ."

Adapted from Genesis 1:31

God put all the wonderful gifts of the earth in our care. He wants us to respect them and to use them in the right way.

We use God's gifts in the right way when we are not wasteful and when we take good care of them. It is right to share them with other people. If we use them properly, we will reach heaven.

Here is a story that tells how some giants and elves used the gifts of the earth:

TALL ELVES AND SMALL GIANTS

The Great King lived in a beautiful castle in the City of Light. Huge giants and tiny elves lived there, too. This city was built on a mountain and stood high above all the lands around it. The City of Light and all other lands belonged to the Great King.

One day the Great King decided to send some of his elves and giants to the Land of Time. He said to them, "Go to the Land of Time and take care of it for me. While you are there, be sure that you can always see the City of Light in the distance. Never let it out of your sight. Then you will use the things that you find there in the right way.

121

"Do not be wasteful with the things in the Land of Time. Share them with one another and take good care of them. When you come back home, you will receive treasures and a special place in my castle."

The elves and the giants were happy to hear this good idea. They said, "We will go, Great King, and do as you say." They marched off to the Land of Time with great joy.

As soon as they arrived, the giants settled in one part and started to use all the good things they found. They forgot what the Great King had said. They became greedy and would not share things with one another. They wasted and destroyed many good things. They stole from one another to get more. Soon, the giants began to shrink, and the things around them hid the City of Light.

The little elves were very wise and remembered what the Great King had said. They used the things in the Land of Time, but they were satisfied with what they had. They shared with one another. They were not wasteful and took good care of everything. They kept their eyes on the City of Light. Everything grew more beautiful, and the elves themselves grew taller. They could see over all the things around them.

One day the Great King called out to the giants and the elves, "Come! It is time to come back home." The giants looked and looked, but they had become so small that they could not see over things around them. They could not find the City of Light. They got lost and were never seen again. The elves had no trouble because they had grown much taller; they could see beyond the things around them. They marched joyfully back to the City of Light and right up to the King's castle. There, they received special places and treasures of gold from the Great King. They lived happily with him forever after.

Use the WORD BANK and fill in the missing words.

WORD BANK
Waste Share
Respect Care

1. We treat the gifts God has given us with _____

2. We _____ God's gifts with others.

3. We do not _____ them.

4. We take good _____ of them.

WE REMEMBER
How do we use the gifts of the earth in the right way?

We use the gifts of the earth in the right way by not wasting them, by taking care of them, and by sharing them with others.

WE RESPOND
Lord, the earth is full of Your goodness. Help me to use the gifts of the earth in the right way.

We Share God's Gifts with Others

We call the earth *our* planet, but the earth and everything in it really belong to God. He has given earth to His creatures to use in order to live and grow. But there are some people in our world who have no homes. Others have no clothing, no food, no medicine, no education.

Some people are poor because they have been treated unfairly. Others are very lonely. They are neither loved nor cared for by anyone.

Many people in the world have not heard the Good News. They need someone to teach them about Jesus.

We belong to God's big family of people with earth as our home. God wants all of His people to be happy. All of us, including people in the future, have a right to earth's gifts. So we must use the riches of earth carefully and wisely. Those of us who have more should share with needy people. When we do this, we show that we are all brothers and sisters in God's family.

Use the code to learn a message from St. Paul that will help you share God's gifts with others.

1	2	3	4	5	6	7
A	C	D	E	F	G	H
8	9	10	11	12	13	14
I	L	O	R	S	U	V

WHAT WILL YOU DO TO HELP OTHERS?
Write your answer on the lines below:

|6|10|3|

|9|10|14|4|12|

|1|

|2|7|4|4|11|5|13|9|

|6|8|14|4|11|

Check the family page for
Theme 22 on page 76.

123

23 WE SPEAK THE TRUTH WITH LOVE

God Wants Us to Speak the Truth

God is always true. He loves the truth. We trust God because everything He says is true. He is always faithful to His promises.

God wants us to tell the truth and to keep our promises. He tells us this in the eighth commandment:

"You shall not bear false witness against your neighbor."

Exodus 20:16

To bear false witness means to tell a lie. God tells us to be truthful always, but especially when we talk about others.

When we tell the truth and keep our promises, we show love for God and for others. Our trust in one another grows. We trust those who tell the truth.

HOW DOES THE TRUTH HELP THE PEOPLE IN THESE PICTURES?

124

Some folks who really know what's true tell tales we like to listen to. We hear them say the strangest things like "trees can talk," and "bears have wings." But though these things are fun to say, we know they really aren't that way.

Color the clouds around the sentences that tease or are just make-believe.

Mark's big brother told him he was going to find a pot of gold at the end a rainbow.

The candy store had chocolate eggs.

Mother told Beth that elves must have made the new dress she found on her favorite doll.

The horse spread his wings and flew over the steep mountain.

The whistle blew to announce the end of the work day.

Mary Jo said she has a pet dinosaur on her farm.

Mike's brother said it was raining cats and dogs.

David loves carrots. His father says, "One day you'll turn into a rabbit."

125

Jesus taught us how important it is to tell the truth. When Jesus was on trial, Pilate asked Him, "Are You a king?" Jesus answered truthfully, even though He knew that He would be put to death because of His reply.

Adapted from John 18:33-37

Sometimes it is not easy to tell the truth. We are tempted to lie to avoid trouble. We are afraid to tell the truth. Sometimes we feel like telling a lie, either to get what we want, or to get out of doing something.

People who tell the truth can be trusted. Jesus gives us the courage to tell the truth and to keep our promises, even when it is hard.

> On the lines below, write a prayer asking Jesus to help you tell the truth.

God Wants Us to Speak with Love

God gave us the wonderful gift of speech.
With this gift we can help others learn.
We can speak to them with love.
We can bring them good news and happiness.

St. Paul wrote a letter to tell how to speak with love.
This is what he said:

When we speak to others, we can make our words like a beautiful song. We do this when we use words that are true, patient, unselfish, and kind. Our words are true when we say what really happened. Our words are patient when we speak softly and hold back angry words. Our words are unselfish when we tell others that we are happy about the good things they do or the nice things they have. Our words are kind and thoughtful when we say polite and friendly things to others.

"I may know many things and speak many languages, but if I do not have love, my words are no more than a noisy gong or a clanging cymbal. Love is always patient and kind. It is not jealous. It does not boast. It is never rude or selfish. Love is never happy with evil, but it is happy with the truth."

Adapted from I Corinthians 13:1, 4-6

WORD BANK

Good work!	How are you?	So long!
Hello!	Please!	Thank you!
May I help you?	I am sorry.	Congratulations!

God wants us to say *only* what is true and good about others. He wants us to protect their good name. Sometimes we show love for others just by being quiet. When someone does something wrong, we show love by not talking about it. If it is something that could hurt the person or somebody else, we show love by telling another person who can help.

God wants us to keep silent about the secrets of our families and of our friends, too. He wants us to say *only* things that will bring happiness and peace to others. Then our words—or our silence—will be like a song with a beautiful melody.

WORD BANK

Song   True
Silent   Unselfish
Kind   Patient
Gong

On the blanks below, write the words that tell how we can use our gift of speech. Use the WORD BANK.

1 Words spoken without love are like a noisy _____.

2 Words spoken with love are like a beautiful _____.

3 Our words should be _____, _____, _____, and _____.

4 Sometimes we should hold back words and be _____.

WE REMEMBER

What is the eighth commandment?
The eighth commandment is:
"You shall not bear false witness against your neighbor."

WE RESPOND

I will speak the truth with love, saying only things that are kind and true.

Check the family page for *Theme 23* on page 77.

Sometimes We Must Suffer for the Truth

Thomas More was a lawyer and a helper to the king of England. The people loved him because he was fair to all, and good to the poor. Thomas prayed at Mass every day and asked God to help him do what was right. He never wanted to offend God.

Henry the Eighth was king when Thomas lived. The king liked Thomas. He knew that Thomas would do whatever he could to help him.

One day, King Henry made himself the head of the Church in England. When Thomas More heard this, he would no longer work for the king. King Henry the Eighth was very angry at Thomas and had him put into prison. But Thomas still would not say that the king was the head of the Church, because it was not true. The judges could not make Thomas say what was not true. They said he must die. Thomas's last words were, "I die as the king's good servant, but God's first."

Work the puzzle about Thomas More. Find the answers in the story above.

M Every day at _____. Thomas prayed for God's help.
O Thomas loved God and would not _____ Him.
R Thomas prayed that God would help him do what was _____.
E Thomas More lived in _____.

24 WE KEEP GOD'S LAWS OF LOVE

We Live God's Laws

A Song about God's Laws
To the melody of "If You're Happy"

O be prayerful and give honor to God's name.
O be prayerful and give honor to God's name.
Then you're happy and you know it,
And your life will surely show it.
O be prayerful and give honor to God's name.

Go to Mass and celebrate the Sabbath day.
Go to Mass and celebrate the Sabbath day.
Then you're happy and you know it,
And your life will surely show it.
Go to Mass and celebrate it on God's day.

Be obedient, kind, and true every day.
Be obedient, kind, and true every day.
Then you're happy and you know it,
And your life will surely show it.
Be obedient, kind, and true every day.

O be faithful and respectful everyday.
O be faithful and respectful everyday.
Then you're happy and you know it.
And your life will surely show it.
O be faithful and respectful everyday.

O be honest and be careful with all things.
O be honest and be careful with all things.
Then you're happy and you know it,
And your life will surely show it.
O be honest and be careful with all things.

We Celebrate God's Laws

SONG   (All sing "A song about God's Laws.")

PRAYER

ALL: Lord God,
          We raise our hearts to You with joy.
          We want to live as You have told us.
          Put Your love into our hearts today.
          Keep us faithful to Your laws.
          We ask this through Jesus our Lord.   Amen.

READING

READER: A reading from a letter of St. Paul.
          All the runners in a race are
          trying to win, but only one gets
          the prize. They do many
          difficult things to train for the
          race. They run very fast to win a
          prize that will not last very long.
          Like the runners, we do difficult
          things as we try to keep God's
          laws. But we do them for a prize
          that will last forever: we will
          reach heaven.

Adapted from 1 Corinthians 9:24-25

          This is the Word of the Lord.

ALL: Thanks be to God.

SILENT PRAYER

AWARDING OF GOLD MEDALS
(Follows comments by the catechist.)

SONG (All sing "Your word, O Lord," or another song.)

> Your Word, O Lord, is the joy of my heart.
> I sing Your praises by night and by day,
> And walk with gladness along Your way.

PRAYER (Individual prayers are said.)

RESPONSE

ALL: Lord, teach us
to love Your laws.

CATECHIST: Let us pray.

CLOSING PRAYER

ALL: Lord, we rejoice because we have Your Laws. They are better than great riches. We will follow them closely. Help us to obey them, O Lord.

SONG (All sing "Julie's Psalm," or another song.)

> Let us sing a song to our Father,
> As we walk along to our Father.
> He is always there,
> God is taking gentle care;
> God is love beyond compare,
> God is good.
>
> To His home above He leads me,
> With His gift of peace He frees me.
> High on angel wings,
> My heart gives Him thanks and sings:
> How He fills us with good things!
> God is good.

Unit 4 Jesus Leads Us to Happiness

The Message of the Unit

Jesus gave us the beatitudes as a guide to Christian living and as a means of obtaining happiness both in this life and in the life to come. By studying the eight beatitudes and applying them in a practical way, the children learn how to live them. They discover how rewarding it can be to follow the examples of Jesus, May, and the saints.
They rejoice with Mary, who was taken body and soul into heaven and was crowned Queen of Heaven and Earth. They honor her by praying the Glorious Mysteries of the rosary, and look forward to meeting her in heaven some day.

Sharing the Message as a Family

Family Pages for Themes in Unit 4

A mark in the box indicates that the theme has been presented in class.

Theme 25: ☐ Happy Are the Poor in Spirit, *pages* 138-144

By giving us the beatitudes, Jesus showed us how to obtain happiness here and hereafter. The first beatitude, "Happy are the poor in spirit; theirs is the kingdom of heaven," advises us to be detached from material things and to be satisfied with what we have. It encourages us to share with others and leads us to trust in God for all our needs.

READ Matthew 6:25-34

DISCUSS
- In Matthew 6:25-34, why does Jesus tell us not to worry about what we will eat or wear? Do Jesus' words in this passage mean that we don't have to work?
- How does our heavenly Father take care of the flowers and the birds?
- Why will God care for us and for our needs?
- What steps can we take as a family toward adopting a simplified life-style?

DO
- Let each family member take a turn completing the phrase, "Happiness is . . ." Which answers fit best with the beatitude, "Happy are the poor in spirit"?
- A slogan very popular in the early years of this century was: "Use it up; wear it out; make it do; do without." Discuss how that slogan could help family members to be "poor in spirit" today. Make up a slogan or motto for your family. (Examples: Be satisfied. Save and share. No complaining allowed.)
- Appoint an older child or an adult to act as secretary and to write all the "blessings of God" which family members can think of in two minutes.
Hold a multifamily rummage sale after spring cleaning and donate the proceeds to a local shelter.
- Consider tithing: donating a percentage of your income to a fund for world hunger.

For Themes 25 to 29:
As a family project, start a "Happiness Book." Use a scrapbook, empty photo album, or a notebook. Allow two pages or a double-faced spread for each beatitude. As each is discussed, print the beatitude at the top of the page, then paste in photos, magazine pictures, or drawings that show how that beatitude is lived. For the first one, "Happy are the poor in spirit; theirs is the kingdom of heaven," you might have pictures like these: a boy with an old baseball mitt, smiling as he passes a store selling new gloves; a mother sewing or re-making a dress for her daughter; a family with an older car, just as happy as the neighbors with their new car; a "Thank-You" card to God for all the blessings He has given your family.

PRAY As a reminder that Jesus wants us to be happy according to His way, say often:
HAPPY ARE WE, O LORD, WHO WALK IN YOUR WAY!

Theme 26 ☐ God's Sorrowing and Lowly People Receive a Special Promise, *pages* 145-150

Suffering is part of everyday life. We accept sorrows and sufferings from the loving hand of God as tools with which He strengthens our faith. By imitating Christ, Who is humble of heart, we meet the challenging situations of life with patience and gentleness.

DISCUSS

- What is the real meaning of the word "gentle" in this passage from Scripture?
- How will "gentle" people possess the earth?
- Why do we suffer? How can we suffer and yet consider ourselves "happy" or "blessed"?
- How does God comfort sorrowing people? How can we comfort them?

READ Matthew 5:4-5

DO

- Add the two beatitudes mentioned so far to the family "Happiness Book."
- Discuss some sufferings or sorrows which your family has recently experienced. Suggest ways for members to comfort one another. (Example: Mother has a headache. Children can "comfort" her by being quiet at work or play.)
- Decide how the family can give help or comfort to a friend or neighbor who is suffering.
- Find and discuss examples of persons who showed real strength by being "gentle" or patient in difficult situations. Tell how those persons can be imitated.

PRAY

When tempted to be impatient or unwilling to suffer, pray:
JESUS, MEEK AND HUMBLE OF HEART, MAKE OUR HEARTS LIKE THINE.

Theme 27 ☐ God's People Long to Be Pure of Heart and Holy, *pages* 151-156

Christ calls us to purity and holiness so that we may share in His happiness. We can attain this sanctity only by seeking God. We seek God when we do all that He desires and when we try to be "pure of heart" like the Blessed Virgin Mary and the saints.

DISCUSS

- What did Jesus say about the "pure of heart"?
- How can we be "pure of heart"?
- What does it mean to be "hungry and thirsty" for holiness?
- Why do we want to please God?

READ Matthew 5:6, 8

DO

- Add the two beatitudes mentioned above to the family "Happiness Book."
- Talk about how each member of the family seeks God in his or her daily routine.
- Examine the TV programs that are viewed by your family. Take steps to eliminate those shows which would be contrary to "purity of heart."
- Which persons living today would you call "holy"? Tell who and why.

PRAY

Call upon Mary, the Blessed Virgin, in time of temptation and say:
MOTHER MOST PURE, PRAY FOR US.

Theme 28: ☐ **God's People Bring Mercy and Peace to Others,** *pages* **157-162**

Our love must embrace all of God's people. By being merciful, we express love and compassion for others. The Holy Spirit's gifts of love and peace enable us to be peacemakers. As such, we try to bring peace into our lives, into our homes, and into the world.

READ
Matthew 5:7,9

DISCUSS

- How did Jesus show mercy to others?
- How can we show mercy to the members of our families? To others?
- Why should we be peacemakers?
- How can we settle problems in peaceful ways?

DO

- Add the two beatitudes mentioned above to the family "Happiness Book."
- Decide as a family which TV shows you will not watch because of the violence they depict. Discuss or comment on violent acts which appear in shows you do view.
- Be a peacemaker: do a good deed toward someone who doesn't seem to like you or to whom you owe a favor.
- Make and maintain a family "Joy Jar." Members write on slips of paper what they will do to bring joy to family members and put them into a "Joy Jar" (a decorated jar). When in need of favors, family members pick a slip and claim the favor. They replace the slip drawn with another of their own. Some ideas are: I will polish your shoes. I will take your turn doing dishes. I will help you with your work for (amount of time).

PRAY

As a reminder that we have an obligation to be peacemakers, say:
LORD, MAKE ME A CHANNEL OF YOUR PEACE:
WHERE THERE IS HATRED, LET ME SOW LOVE.

READ
Matthew 5:10-12

Theme 29: ☐ **Jesus Leads Us to Happiness,** *pages* **163-169**

God brings good out of evil, and happiness out of suffering. We learn this especially when we ponder the crucifixion of Christ. Jesus enjoyed the glory of the resurrection only after great suffering. With His grace, we can have the courage to bear suffering. In so doing, we keep in mind the example of the martyrs and the happiness promised to us by Jesus.

DISCUSS

- Why are we expected to suffer in this world?
- How should we accept suffering when it comes into our lives?
- What should we do to prepare ourselves for suffering?
- How can we help others who suffer?

DO

- Add the beatitude, "Happy are they who suffer for what is right; the kingdom of heaven is theirs," to the family "Happiness Book."
- With the family, discuss ways of bearing up under mental or physical suffering. How can we train ourselves to accept suffering or persecution?
- Read stories about the martyrs from a missal or from a book about saints. How do their sufferings compare with yours?
- Sometimes we are persecuted for doing the right thing. Why is the following motto a challenge: "Dare to do right, even if nobody else is doing it!"

PRAY

Look at the crucifix, think of what Jesus suffered, and say:
LORD JESUS, I ACCEPT ALL AS YOUR WILL.
HELP ME BEAR ALL WITH YOU AND FOR YOU.

Theme 30: ☐ We Rejoice with Mary, *pages* 170-175

We rejoice with Mary, who was chosen by God to be the mother of His Son. Because she was faithful to all that God asked of her, she was taken body and soul into heaven when she died. There, she was crowned Queen of Heaven and Earth. She prays for us so that we, too, may one day enjoy the happiness of heaven.

DISCUSS
- What is the meaning of Mary's Queenship?
- Why is Mary our greatest intercessor?
- Why do we meditate on the Glorious Mysteries of the rosary?
- Why is Mary honored under so many different titles?

READ Luke 1: 26-56

DO
- Pray the family rosary, meditating especially on the Glorious Mysteries. Take turns mentioning a few thoughts about each mystery.
- Plan a family pilgrimage to a shrine of Mary. (It doesn't have to be one that is nationally known. Some are connected with parish churches.)
- Have a picture or statue of Mary in a place of honor in your home. Decorate it in an appropriate way.
- Make a special "Mary Calendar" of various feasts of Our Lady, or mark the feasts on a write-in calendar. Celebrate each feast in a special way to show love for Mary. Family members could take turns suggesting different ways of honoring Mary: saying the rosary together, doing a special deed in honor of Mary, celebrating Eucharist together, if possible, or having a Day of Kindness in her honor.
- Start a collection of pictures, poems, prayers, favorite readings, and other clippings about Mary. These could be kept in envelopes until enough are collected, then put in a scrapbook or photo album. This "Mary Book" could be an on-going family project.
- Since this is the last family page, you might like to get together with another family or two from your child's class to share projects, activities, and results of discussions; then possibly end your meeting with a brief prayer service and simple refreshments.

PRAY

As a tribute to Mary and to ask her help, say:
HAIL, HOLY QUEEN, MOTHER OF LOVE
HELP US REACH OUR HOME ABOVE!

25 HAPPY ARE THE POOR IN SPIRIT

Jesus Showed Us the Way to Happiness

While He was on earth, Jesus was very happy. He was happy because He loved God and always did what pleased His Father.

Jesus was happy even though He knew He would suffer. He was happy even though He was poor. He showed us that happiness is not found in having many things, and that it is not found in having only pleasant things happen to us.

Jesus wants us all to share His happiness. To help us live in hope and love, He gave us the eight beatitudes.

THE BEATITUDES

**Happy are the poor in spirit;
the kingdom of heaven is theirs.**

**Happy are the sorrowing;
they will be comforted.**

**Happy are the lowly;
they will own the land.**

**Happy are they who hunger and thirst to be holy;
they will be filled.**

**Happy are they who show mercy;
they will receive mercy.**

**Happy are the pure of heart;
they will see God.**

**Happy are the peacemakers;
they will be called children of God.**

Happy are they who suffer for what is right; the kingdom of heaven is theirs.

Adapted from Matthew 5:3-10

This puzzle will tell you the name of Jesus' way to happiness. Use the code below and print the letters in the puzzle.

A	B	D	E	I	S	T	U
△	▭	▷	⌣	⊙	✳	⊥	✝

▭	⌣	△	⊥	⊙	⊥	✝	▷	⌣	✳

WE REMEMBER

What do we call the way to happiness that Jesus gave us?

We call Jesus' way to happiness the beatitudes.

WE RESPOND

How happy those who seek the Lord with their whole heart.

Adapted from Psalm 119:2

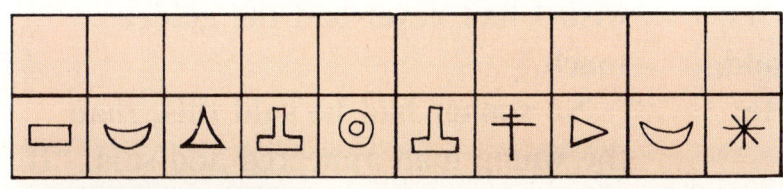

139

King Midas and the Golden Touch

This is a story about a king who loved gold. Read it to find out what he learned about riches.

King Midas loved gold very much. He loved it almost as much as he loved his little girl, Marigold. One day, the king made a strange wish. He said, "I wish everything I touch would turn into gold." At that moment, a young man came to him and said, "Tomorrow morning your wish will be granted."

What a surprise King Midas had the next morning! When he awoke, he found his bed had turned to gold! As he dressed, his clothes turned to gold, too. His wish had been granted! He had been given the golden touch!

The king hurried from room to room in the palace changing everything he saw into gold. To surprise Princess Marigold, who loved the flower garden, he changed each flower into a bright, shining, golden blossom. "How pleased Marigold will be!" thought the king.

Feeling very happy about what he had done, King Midas went inside the palace to eat his breakfast. How beautiful the table appeared with all its golden plates, glasses, and cups! The king then sat down to eat. Each thing that he tried to eat turned to gold!

"Oh! What will I do now?" thought the king. Before he could think of an answer, he was startled by the sound of Marigold's voice.

"Oh, father," she cried, "all our beautiful flowers have turned into gold!" Gently the king tried to comfort her. Forgetting about his golden touch, he put his arms around her. At that instant, Princess Marigold became a hard, golden statue.

"Oh, no!" cried the king in horror. "How foolish I have been! I have lost my Marigold, the one I love most. I wish I had never had the golden touch."

No sooner had he said this, than the young man appeared and said, "If you wish to lose the golden touch, you must sprinkle everything with water from the river."

Quickly the king did as he was told. Soon his beloved Marigold, the garden, and all of the other things were just as they were before he was given the golden touch.

In this way, King Midas learned that all the gold in the world did not make him happy.

141

Like King Midas, people are foolish when they think that riches can bring them happiness. If we remember that Jesus told us to love God above everything, we can be "poor in spirit." To be "poor in spirit" means to realize that we are always in need of God's help. It is to be satisfied with having what we need, to be grateful for God's gifts, to share them with others. When we do these things, we will have the happiness that Jesus promised when He said:

"Happy are the poor in spirit;
the kingdom of heaven is theirs."

Adapted from Matthew 5:3

> Tell how the children in the following stories are being "poor in spirit." Use the WORD BANK to write the correct word on each line.

1. Cindy received a new bike for Christmas. She took it over to show Ann. Ann was happy for Cindy. But Ann was just as happy with her own gift, a doll. Ann was "poor in spirit" because she was _____.

2. Craig planned to use the money he earned to buy a new baseball. At Sunday Mass a missionary asked help for hungry people in the missions. Craig gave part of his money. He was "poor in spirit" because he was _____.

3. Mr. and Mrs. Peters own a large department store. They live in a beautiful house with a big lawn. Every morning before going to their store, Mr. and Mrs. ask God to help them be honest and fair to their customers. They are "poor in spirit" because they show they _____.

4. Jane's parents are divorced, and her mother has to work. Jane doesn't have a lot of things, but she always has clean clothes and enough food to eat. She has many persons who love her. At night Jane thanks God for taking care of her mother and herself. She is "poor in spirit" because she shows she is _____.

WORD BANK

generous
grateful
satisfied
need God

WE REMEMBER

What did Jesus say about the poor in spirit? Jesus said, "Happy are the poor in spirit;
the kingdom of heaven is theirs."

WE RESPOND

Listen to me, Lord, and answer me, poor and needy as I am.

Adapted from Psalm 86:1

Check the family page for *Theme 25* on page 134.

ST. FRANCIS, "GOD'S LITTLE POOR MAN"

Francis was a very rich young man who lived in the little Italian town of Assisi. His father, who had a good business, wanted Francis to follow in his footsteps. But God had other plans; He called Francis to follow the example of His Son, Jesus.

One time, Francis met a poor man who was dressed in rags. He felt so sorry for the man that he exchanged clothes with him. The poor man walked away wearing Francis' fine coat, belt, and sandals. When Francis put on the poor man's ragged clothes, he felt the happiness promised to those who are poor in spirit.

The Holy Spirit led Francis to understand that he could show his love for Jesus by giving up his riches. So, one day, Francis left all that he owned and began to live as a poor man.

He did not miss his worldly riches, because he loved God above all things. He saw God's love and care in everything around him. St. Francis wanted to share God's love with others. Most of all, he wanted to share it with the hungry, poor, and sad people in the world. He wanted to bring happiness to them by sharing food, clothing, and his joy with them all.

> On the line below, fill in the word that tells what we will want to do if we are "poor in spirit."

_____

If we are "poor in spirit," we will _____ with others.

Canticle of the Sun

by St. Francis of Assisi

Be praised, my Lord,
For all Your creatures,
For Brother Sun,
For Sister Moon,
And for the stars.

Be praised for Brother Wind,
For the air,
For the clouds,
And for all kinds of weather.

Be praised for Sister Water,
Who is so useful and
lovely and pure.

Be praised for Brother Fire,
Who is so beautiful, bright,
and strong.

Be praised for Mother Earth,
Who gives us fruit
and plants and flowers.

Be praised for those
who serve You
And forgive others
for love of You.

Praise and bless the Lord,
all you children,
Serve Him and
give Him thanks.

26 GOD'S SORROWING AND LOWLY PEOPLE RECEIVE A SPECIAL PROMISE

Sorrowing People Will Be Comforted

By His life, Jesus taught us to trust that God our Father will bring good from all our sorrows. In one of the beatitudes, He promised a special peace to sorrowing or suffering people. He said:

"Happy are the sorrowing; they will be comforted."

Adapted from Matthew 5:5

Jesus had sorrows and sufferings, just as we do. But He put all His trust in God our Father. When He suffered in the garden on the night before He died, He prayed:

"Father, if it is possible, take this suffering away from Me! But let it be as You, not I, would wish."

Adapted from Matthew 26:39

Jesus knew that His death on the cross would save us. He knew that, in heaven, God would change His sorrows into joy.

Mary became our "Mother of Sorrows" because she suffered so much when she stood at the foot of the cross. But her sorrow was changed into joy when Jesus rose from the dead.

Jesus let us know that His followers would have to suffer, too. He said:

"Take up your cross and follow Me."

Adapted from Mark 8:34

But in the beatitudes, He promises that if we accept our sufferings willingly, we will be happy because we will be comforted. In heaven, God will change all our sorrows into a joy that will never end.

Jesus felt sorry for people who were suffering. Once, He looked out over the beautiful city of Jerusalem. He saw that many people suffered because they did not believe in Him. He began to weep and said:

"If only you knew the way to happiness! But you have lost sight of it. Now your enemies will take your city, because you did not believe in the Savior."

Adapted from Luke 19:41-44

Jesus did all He could to help suffering people. He prayed for them, taught them, and forgave them. He even gave His life to save them.

God's people feel sorry when they see others suffer. They feel sad when they see that others are unhappy because they do not know or love Jesus. They pray and offer sacrifices to bring these people to Him.

There is a legend about a holy woman named Veronica. The legend says that Veronica felt sorry when she saw Jesus carrying the heavy cross. She tried to comfort Him by wiping His face with her veil. Jesus was so pleased that He left the picture of His face on her veil.

Jesus wants us to help those who suffer. Even though it may be sad for us or difficult, He wants us to help them with kindness, our prayers, and our sacrifices. By showing love and concern for others, we show our love for Jesus. We show that we belong to God's people.

If we do this, Jesus will give us a greater share in His life and love. When we arrive in heaven, we will find that He has changed all our sorrows into joy!

It's not easy to be one of God's sorrowing people. Jesus tells us what to do when we have sorrow.

On the blanks below, print the letter of the alphabet that comes before each letter that is shown. Then you will find out what Jesus tells us to do when we are sad.

"D P N F   U P
_ _ _ _   _ _

N F   B O E
_ _   _ _ _

J X J M M
_ _ _ _ _

H J W F
_ _ _ _

Z P V
_ _ _

S F T U."
_ _ _ _

Adapted from Matthew 11:28

147

Lowly People Are Humble and Gentle

One fine day Mr. Wind bragged to Mr. Sun that he was stronger. Mr. Wind stuck out his chest, held his head high, and said, "I am stronger than you, Mr. Sun. I can blow over trees and raise a lot of dust. I can blow ships across the ocean. I can make howling noise that can be heard for miles around."

Mr. Sun smiled brightly and replied in his quiet voice, "Let's have a contest to see which of us is stronger. Do you see that man coming down the street wearing a heavy coat? Let's see which of us can make the man take off his coat. That will show which of us is stronger. You may have the first try."

So Mr. Wind blew with all his might. He became angry and made a howling noise. The harder and longer he blew, the tighter the man gripped his coat. Finally, Mr. Wind became very tired and gave up.

Then Mr. Sun took this turn. He came out slowly from behind the clouds and let one hot ray after another fall gently upon the man. At first the man unbuttoned his coat. Before long he grew very hot and exclaimed: "Wow! Is it ever hot! I must take off this coat." And that is just what he did.

Mr. Sun smiled at Mr. Wind, who had calmed down to a gentle breeze. Never again did Mr. Wind brag to Mr. Sun that he was stronger.

In one of the beatitudes, Jesus spoke about lowly people. He said:
"Happy are the lowly;
they will own the land."

Adapted from Matthew 5:4

Lowly people are not at all like Mr. Wind in the story. He bragged about himself and became angry. Lowly people are more like the gentle Mr. Sun. They are like Jesus, Who said:
"Learn from Me,
for I am gentle
and humble of heart."

Adapted from Matthew 11:29

Use the WORD BANK to fill in the missing words in the sentences below. They will tell you how you can become more gentle and humble.

WORD BANK

quiet   pray
praise   serve
patient   forgive

1. Be _____ when people do not understand you.

2. When you are upset, be _____ until you can answer kindly.

3. When someone says or does unkind things, _____ that person.

4. When others need help, be ready to _____ them.

5. When others play a good game and win, _____ them.

6. _____ for grace to control harmful feelings.

149

When Francis de Sales was a boy, he often became angry. Because he sometimes hurt himself and others by losing his temper, he decided to ask Jesus to help him whenever he felt himself getting angry or upset. He would make up for hurting someone by doing something kind for that person.

With God's help, Francis became such a kind and gentle man that people could hardly believe that he once had a hot temper. Today we know him as St. Francis de Sales.

When we are gentle and humble like Jesus, Mary, and the saints, we show that we understand what Jesus said about lowly people.

Draw a ☺ if the sentence tells about some way in which you can be gentle or humble. Draw a ☹ if it does not.

○ Say, "I'm sorry. Please forgive me."

○ Let someone have the first turn doing something you like.

○ Say, "You really did a good job."

○ Push yourself ahead of someone in line.

○ Pout when someone else wins a game.

○ Share something you like.

○ Offer to do a chore for someone.

○ Pray for someone who has been unkind to you.

WE REMEMBER

What did Jesus say about the sorrowing and the lowly?
"Happy are the sorrowing;
 they will be comforted."
"Happy are the lowly;
 they will own the land."

WE RESPOND

Jesus, gentle and humble of heart, make my heart like Yours.

Check the family page for *Theme 26* on page 134.

27 GOD'S PEOPLE LONG TO BE PURE OF HEART AND HOLY

The Pure of Heart Will See God

The pure of heart are God's happy people. Jesus spoke of them when He said:

"Happy are the pure of heart; they will see God."

Adapted from Matthew 5:8

Jesus was pure of heart. His heart was filled with love for His Father. He saw God our Father in everything, and everyone saw the Father's love in Him. He gave glory to the Father by His whole life and by His death on the cross.

Mary was pure of heart, too. She was free from sin. From the moment God made her, she belonged entirely to Him. Her heart was full of love. She pleased God in everything she did. She thought of others and made them happy. Now Mary is with God in heaven, where she sees Him in all His beauty and glory. Mary will help us to be pure of heart. We can say to her,

"Mother most pure, pray for us."

> Finish the beatitude by naming the reward the "pure of heart" will have.

"Happy are the pure of heart; _____ _____
- - - - - - - - -
they will _____ _____."

Many years ago, there lived in Italy a boy named Aloysius. He belonged to a rich family and had everything he wanted. One summer, when he was seven, his father took him to a camp where soldiers trained. Aloysius picked up some bad words from these men. After he returned home, he happened to say these words one day in school. When his teacher scolded him for this, Aloysius learned how wrong it was to offend God, even in a small way. From that time on, he was careful not to say or do anything that would offend God or hurt others. He tried to please God and to keep his heart pure.

Aloysius grew in love for God by praying to Him often during the day. He loved the psalms and prayed them. He said special prayers to Mary each day. Once, he went to a shrine of Mary in the city of Florence. When he knelt before the beautiful statue of Mary, he was filled with a great desire to be pure and holy. He wanted to serve God always and to please our Blessed Mother. He promised God he would never sin and asked Mary to help him. He often went to church to pray and was happy when he could receive Jesus in Holy Communion.

Aloysius loved Jesus so much that he decided to give himself to Jesus in a special way by becoming a priest. He left his rich home and all his money to become a member of the Society of Jesus.

Color the medal of Mary to make it more beautiful.

Make a design around the back of the medal. Print the words *Mother most pure, pray for us* on the lines.

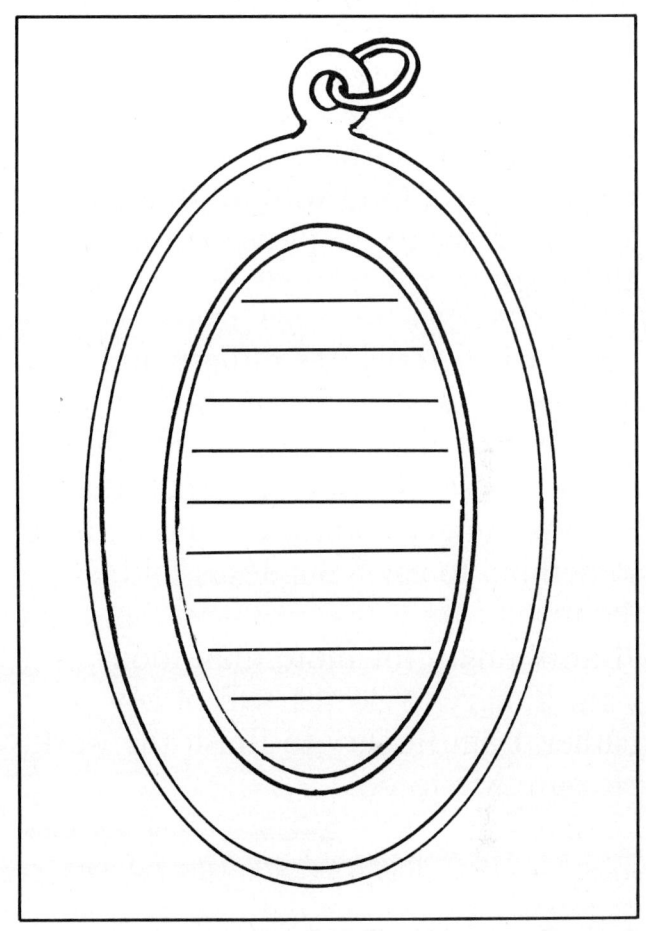

While Aloysius was studying in Rome to be a priest, a terrible disease broke out in the city. Aloysius helped care for the sick until he became sick himself. After suffering for three months, he died at the age of twenty-three. Now Aloysius is with God in heaven, where he sees Him in all His glory. He has received the wonderful reward Jesus promised to the pure of heart.

We, too, can become pure of heart like Jesus, Mary, and the saints. When our hearts are pure, we are able to see God in the beautiful world around us. We are able to see Him in ourselves and in other people. One day, we will see God in heaven. We can ask Mary and St. Aloysius to pray for us.

WE REMEMBER

What did Jesus say about the pure of heart?
"Happy are the pure of heart; they will see God."

WE RESPOND

God, create a pure heart in me.

Adapted from Psalm 51:10

We Hunger and Thirst to Be Holy

Jesus told us about people who desire to be holy. He said:
"Happy are they who hunger and thirst to be holy; they will be filled."

Adapted from Matthew 5:6

We show our desire to be holy when we try to love God with all our heart and when we try to please Him in all things.

Once, when Jesus was hungry and thirsty, He went to a well. After a woman had given Him a drink, He sat down to rest. His disciples knew that He was hungry and said, "Master, have something to eat." But Jesus told them:
"I am hungry for more than food. I am hungry to do the will of My Father. I am hungry to finish the work He gave Me to do."

Adapted from John 4:5-34

Jesus loved His Father so much that He tried to please Him in everything. He pleased His Father when he obeyed His parents. He showed love for His Father when He prayed to Him.
He prayed alone on the mountain.
He prayed with others in the temple.

Jesus did the work His Father wanted Him to do. He told people how much God Our Father loved them. He healed the sick. He forgave persons who were sorry for their sins. He finished His Father's work when He suffered and died on the Cross to gain heaven for all of us.

MARY'S GREATEST DESIRE

Mary was holy. She loved God so much that her greatest desire was to do His will. When the angel told her that God wanted her to be the mother of Jesus, she said, "Be it done to me as you have said."

Adapted from Luke 1:38

Mary was happy because she always did what God wished. Now she is happy with God in heaven. We pray to her:
"Holy Mary, Mother of God, pray for us."

THERESA'S DESIRE

Even as a little girl, Theresa wanted to be holy. She knew that to become a saint, one not only had to love God very much, but one also had to suffer like Jesus.

She also understood that she was free to sacrifice much or little for Jesus. But Theresa loved Jesus so much that she told Him, "I choose everything You want me to do. I am not afraid to suffer for You."

All her life, Theresa made many sacrifices for Jesus. She always tried to be like Him. Once, she said, "My heart does not wish for riches or glory. What I ask for is love. Only one thing, my Jesus, to love You."

Now Theresa is with God in heaven. She is filled with His love.

WISHING ON A STAR

We're wishing, Lord, upon a star,

To be as holy as You are.

We're seeking, God, just to do

The things that please

and honor You.

DOMINIC SAVIO'S DESIRE

As a very young boy, Dominic Savio wished with all his heart to become holy. He had learned all his prayers by heart by the time he was five years old. When he received his First Communion at the age of seven, he told God about his one great desire. It was, "Death before sin." By this, Dominic meant that he loved God so much, he would rather die than commit a sin.

> Here is a puzzle. The word going down spells DESIRE. Fill in the words going across. Use the clues and WORD BANK.

D God's _____ tells us how to be holy.

E A desire to be holy is like a _____.

S A desire is a strong _____.

I We want to do God's _____.

R We can be _____ for holiness.

E To become holy, we must give God our _____.

To Dominic, death meant that he would at last see God, Whom he loved above all else. When Dominic was only fifteen years old, God took him to heaven. There, he and all the other saints enjoyed God's life and love. They are filled with a happiness that will last forever.

If we hunger and thirst to be holy, we, too, will be filled with a happiness that will never end.

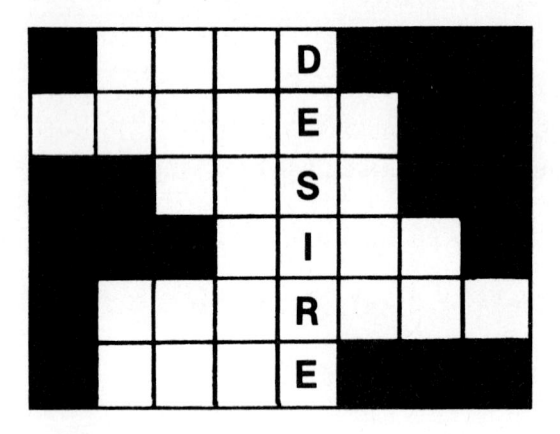

WORD BANK

wish	Word
will	hunger
love	thirsty

WE REMEMBER

What did Jesus say about those who hunger and thirst to be holy? "Happy are they who hunger and thirst to be holy; they will be filled."

WE RESPOND

Taste and see how good the Lord is. Those who seek him lack nothing good.

Adapted from Psalm 34:8-10

Check the family page for *Theme 27* on perform-a-text page 135.

28 GOD'S PEOPLE BRING MERCY AND PEACE TO OTHERS

God's Merciful People Will Receive Mercy

In another beatitude, Jesus tells us: "Happy are they who show mercy; they will receive mercy."

Adapted from Matthew 5:7

Jesus was merciful, just like His Father. When He was dying on the cross, He said, "Father, forgive them; they do not know what they are doing."

Adapted from Luke 23:34

Our Blessed Mother was merciful when Jesus died on the cross. She, too, forgave His enemies. We call Mary the "Mother of Mercy." She helps those in need.

Jesus told us how to show mercy. He said:

"Be merciful as your heavenly Father is merciful. Love your enemies. Do good to those who hate you and pray for them. Give to those who are in need. Give them even more than they need. Do not wish for anything in return. Forgive, and you will be forgiven. Give to others, and it shall be given back to you."

Adapted from Luke 6:27-38

Find out what Jesus said about people who show mercy. The clues below will help you work the puzzle.

Down:
1 Merciful people _____ those who hurt them.
2 They do _____ to those who hate them.
3 They _____ their enemies.

Across:
2 Merciful people _____ to everyone in need.
4 They _____ for those who hate them.

Frances Cabrini was one of God's merciful people. She wanted to help everyone. She left Italy to be a missionary sister in the United States. Great numbers of people from her country had moved to America hoping to find a better life. But many of them were suffering because they could not find jobs. They had to live in very poor places and go without the food and clothes they needed. Many became weak and ill.

Mother Cabrini and her sisters begged for food and clothing for these people. They started hospitals, homes for children, and schools. Mother Cabrini prayed that she always walk in the footsteps of Jesus.

Before Mother Cabrini died, she became an American citizen. Now she is St. Frances Cabrini, the first United States citizen to be named a saint.

Historical Pictures Service, Chicago

Errand of Mercy

GAME

Use dice and markers for this game. Throw the dice and move a marker as many spaces as the dice tell you. Write the number on the SCORE CARD. If you land on a space that tells about an act of mercy, you may add the number given there to your score. Each player gets six turns; the one with the highest score wins.

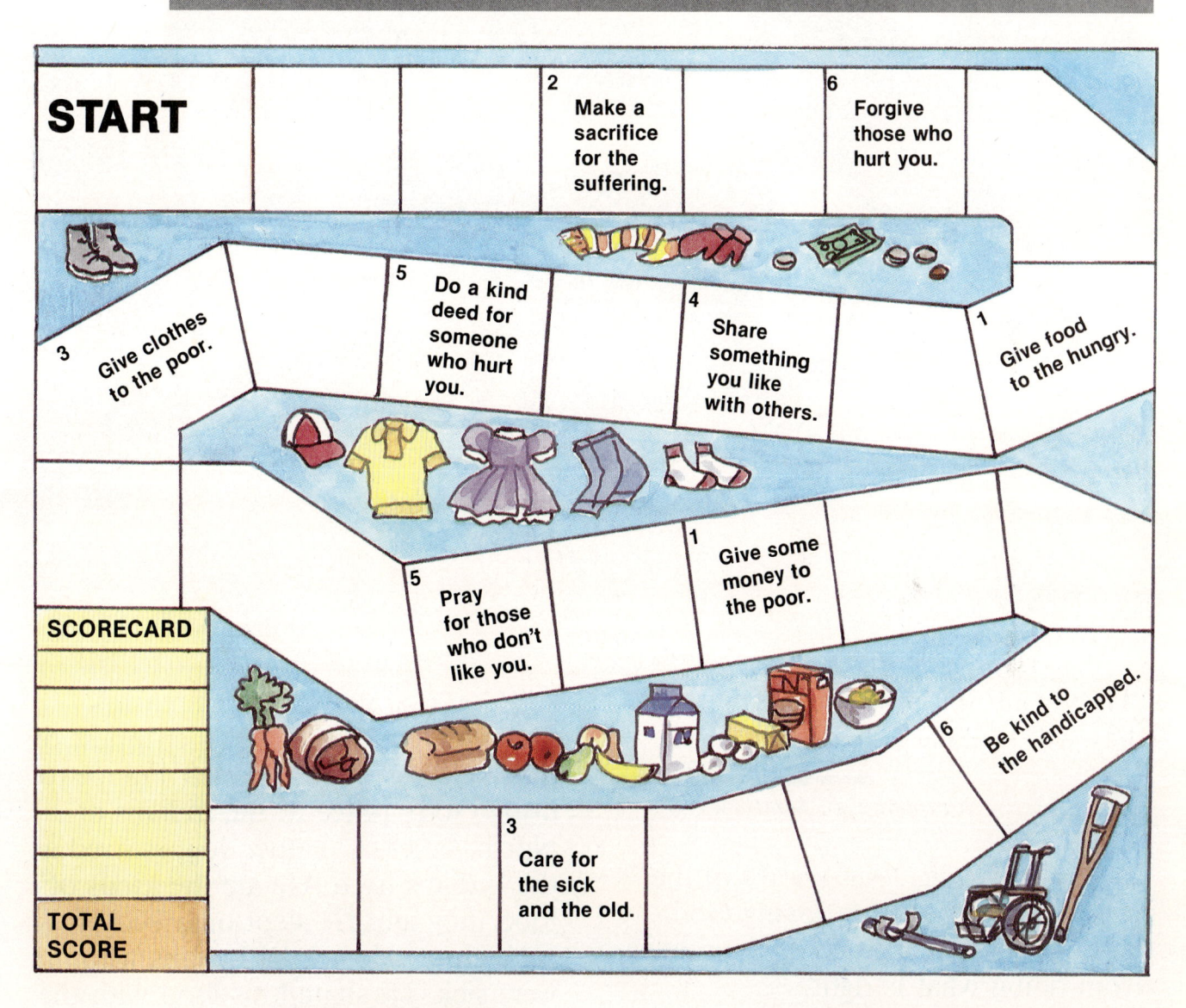

START

- 2 Make a sacrifice for the suffering.
- 6 Forgive those who hurt you.
- 3 Give clothes to the poor.
- 5 Do a kind deed for someone who hurt you.
- 4 Share something you like with others.
- 1 Give food to the hungry.
- 5 Pray for those who don't like you.
- 1 Give some money to the poor.
- 6 Be kind to the handicapped.
- 3 Care for the sick and the old.

SCORECARD

TOTAL SCORE

WE REMEMBER

What did Jesus say about people who are merciful? "Happy are they who show mercy; they will receive mercy."

WE RESPOND

Lord, help me to forgive others and to show mercy.

159

God's Children Are Peacemakers

"Happy are the peacemakers;
they will be called children of God."

Adapted from Matthew 5:9

In this beatitude, Jesus speaks of the peace that comes from loving God and others. It is a peace that comes from doing what is right.

God sent Jesus into the world to give us His peace. Jesus often greeted His apostles by saying, "Peace be to you." He showed us the way to peace.

Mary's heart was full of God's peace. We call her the "Queen of Peace" and ask her to help us live in peace.

All God's saints were peacemakers. St. Isaac Jogues was a French priest of the Society of Jesus. He left France to bring God's peace to the Indians of North America. Father Jogues lived as the Indians lived. He ate the kinds of food they ate. He slept on a bed of bark chips. He helped Indians who were sick. He shared his food with the Indians when they were hungry.

Father Jogues and other missionaries often sat down with their Indian friends to smoke the peace pipe. Smoking the peace pipe was a sign that they could trust one another. One tribe of Indians would not smoke the peace pipe with the French. This tribe captured Isaac Jogues. They made him their prisoner and were cruel to him. But Father Jogues prayed for them. He taught them about God's love and even baptized some of them. He offered his sufferings to God for them.

One day Father Jogues escaped and went back to France. He was so thin and sick that his friends did not know him. As soon as he was well, he went back to Canada to work with the Indians again. He tried to help enemy tribes make peace with one another. Father Jogues even went to help the Indians who had treated him so cruelly. He had forgiven them.

One night, an Indian in the camp invited Father Jogues to his home for supper. As Father Jogues entered the tent, another Indian struck him with his tomahawk and killed him. Isaac Jogues, God's peacemaker, died a martyr for Jesus.

WE CAN DO THINGS TO MAKE PEACE

Read each story and underline what each child could do to bring God's peace to others.

1. At supper Jean's brother Pat told the family that Jean had been scolded on the playground because she played after the bell rang. Jean felt embarrassed and was angry at Pat. When their father told Pat he should not have said what he did, Pat said he was sorry. But the evening meal was unpleasant because everyone felt Jean's anger. What should Jean do?

   Tell something mean about Pat. Forgive Pat. Keep being angry.

2. Linda's little sister Anita took the best dress Linda had for her doll. She tried to put it on her teddy bear and tore it. When Linda came home from school, she saw Anita in tears and the torn doll dress. What should Linda do?

   Tell Anita she can fix it. Scold her. Slap her hands.

3. Joan saw that her baby brother had left his toys all over the floor. She knew her mother would not like such a mess. What should she do?

   Leave them where they are. Tell her mother. Pick them up.

4. Mike went out to play at recess with the other boys. He wanted to play a game of "Keep Away." The other boys wanted to play "kick ball." What should Mike do?

   Quarrel with the boys. Play "kick ball." Refuse to play.

PRAYER FOR PEACE

Here is a prayer said to be written by St. Francis, "God's Little Poor Man." Pray it often.

Lord, make me an instrument
 of Your peace.
Where there is hatred, let me
 bring love;
Where there is injury, pardon;
Where there is doubt, faith;
Where there is despair, hope;
Where there is darkness, light;
Where there is sadness, joy.

WE REMEMBER

What did Jesus say about peacemakers? "Happy are the peacemakers; they will be called children of God."

WE RESPOND

Lord, make me an instrument of your peace.

Check the family page for *Theme 28* on page 136.

29 JESUS LEADS US TO HAPPINESS

God's People Suffer for Him

Jesus told His followers that He loved them so much, He was happy to suffer and die for them. He told them to love others as He did and not to be afraid. He said:

"Some people will make you suffer because of My name. They may even put you to death. I will be with you and I will help you."

Adapted from Luke 21:12-17

In one of the beatitudes, Jesus spoke about those who would suffer for Him. He said:

"Happy are they who suffer for what is right; the kingdom of heaven is theirs."

Adapted from Matthew 5:10

Our Blessed Mother loved and suffered as Jesus did. We call her the "Queen of Martyrs." The saints loved as Jesus did. Those who suffered and died for Jesus are martyrs.

WE REMEMBER

What did Jesus say about those who suffer for what is right? "Happy are they who suffer for what is right; the kingdom of heaven is theirs."

WE RESPOND

Jesus, give me the courage to do what is right even when I must suffer for it.

Check the family page for *Theme 29* on page 136.

WORD BANK

Mary   yes
right   reward
ask   treat

Use the WORD BANK and the clues to fill in the puzzle.

M _____ is the Queen of Martyrs.

A We _____ Jesus to help us suffer bravely.

R The kingdom of heaven will be our _____.

T We must _____ others kindly.

Y We should say _____ to what God wants us to do.

R We must be willing to suffer for what is _____.

ST. JOAN OF ARC

Joan of Arc was a brave girl who lived in a village in France. At the time she lived, her country was at war with England. The king of France was weak and did not think his armies could save France. Joan began hearing the voices of saints urging her to save her country. She said that St. Michael the Archangel told her, "Daughter of God, go and save France." Some of God's saints also told Joan she must save her country.

Although Joan was afraid, she did what God wanted. Carrying a banner, she led the French army into battle. On the banner were written the names of Jesus and Mary. Joan won some battles that helped to save France.

Many people did not believe that God spoke to Joan in a special way. They called her a "witch" and other wicked names. But Joan kept on doing what she thought was right.

Soon, she was captured by the enemy and put into prison. Although she was treated very unfairly, she forgave and prayed for her enemies. When she was put to death by fire, her last word was "Jesus." Joan suffered very bravely for God and for her country. Today, we call her St. Joan of Arc.

> Print the names of Jesus and Mary on St. Joan's banner.

INTRODUCTION

In the eight beatitudes, Jesus calls us to the greatest happiness—joy in the Lord. He and His blessed Mother have shown us the way. The saints who followed their example found happiness both in this life and in heaven. Jesus wants us to be happy now and always.

SONG

We Are Glad

LEADER:

St. Paul was happy like Jesus. He taught the early Christians what they must do to have joy in the Lord. *(Please be seated.)*

FIRST READING

A reading from a letter of St. Paul. I want you to be happy in the Lord always. Yes, it is your happiness that I want. Be glad, and let everyone see that you are unselfish. Be gentle and merciful to all. The Lord will come and you will rejoice with Him forever. Do not worry. If you need anything, pray for it with thankful hearts. Then you will be filled with the peace and happiness of Christ.
This is the Word of the Lord.

Adapted from Philippians 4:4-7

RESPONSE:

Thanks be to God.

SONG

in the Lord

RESPONSE

LEADERS:

That we may become poor in spirit and be happy to share with others...

That we may try to help those who are sorrowing...

That we may become gentle and more willing to serve others...

That we may become holy by loving God with all our hearts...

That we may be forgiving and show mercy to those in need...

That we may be pure of heart by loving God and others...

That we may become peacemakers for God and for others...

That we may be strong enough to suffer for what is right...

ALL:

Stay with us, Lord, and be our joy.

LEADER:

Let us listen to what St. Paul says about a glad heart.

SECOND READING

A reading from a letter of St. Paul. If a man plants a few seeds, he will have a small garden. If he plants many seeds, he will have a large garden. Be generous, then, when you give. Do not give sadly or grudgingly. Give with a glad heart, because God loves a cheerful giver.
This the Word of the Lord.

Adapted from 2 Corinthians 9:6-7

RESPONSE: Thanks be to God.

SILENT PRAYER ON THE PICTURES

Read about the child in each picture to find out why they look different.

This child gave little sadly.

This child gave much cheerfully.

Ask Jesus to help you be a cheerful and generous giver.

THIRD READING

A reading from the Book of Revelation.

Jesus will come again at the end of time. God's children will see Him face to face. For them it will never be dark again. They will not need a lamp or the sun to give them light. Jesus says: "I am coming soon. Happy are they who keep My words. I will reward each one for what he or she did. Happy are they who have the life of grace. To them, the Holy Spirit will say, 'Come.' They will be able to come through the city gates."
These are the words of the Lord.

Adapted from Revelation 22:4-20

RESPONSE: Thanks be to God.

PSALM PRAYER

ALL:
Clap your hands, all you children,
Sing to God with songs of joy,
For He is the Lord of all,
The King of heaven and earth.
The Lord is King of all the earth,
Let the trumpets blast with joy,
Play and sing hymns of praise to God,
Sing praise to our Lord and King.

Adapted from Psalm 47

LEADER:
Jesus gave us a way to live in hope and love when He gave us the eight beatitudes. He has blessed us with happiness in this celebration. Let us thank Him and think of things we can do to make others happy today. Let us tell Jesus what we shall do.

SILENT PRAYER

SONG

We Review the Way to Happiness

A HAPPY HEART PUZZLE

Work this puzzle. Use the clues and the WORD BANK.

Across:

1   Jesus said, "_____ be to you."

5   We should be _____ like our heavenly Father.

6   We become _____ by doing God's will.

7   We can write the word "saint" in this way: _____.

8   The saint who fought for France was St. Joan of _____.

Down:

1   The kingdom of heaven belongs to the _____ in spirit.

2   God's sorrowing people will receive _____.

3   We please God when we do what is _____.

4   Sometimes Christians must _____ for the name of Jesus.

WORD BANK

merciful
comfort
suffer
right
poor
holy
Peace
Arc
St.

In this frame, draw a picture of something you will do to make others happy.

THE CITY OF H__A__E__

A SURPRISE PICTURE

Connect the dots by number. Print the missing letters in the title. Color the picture.

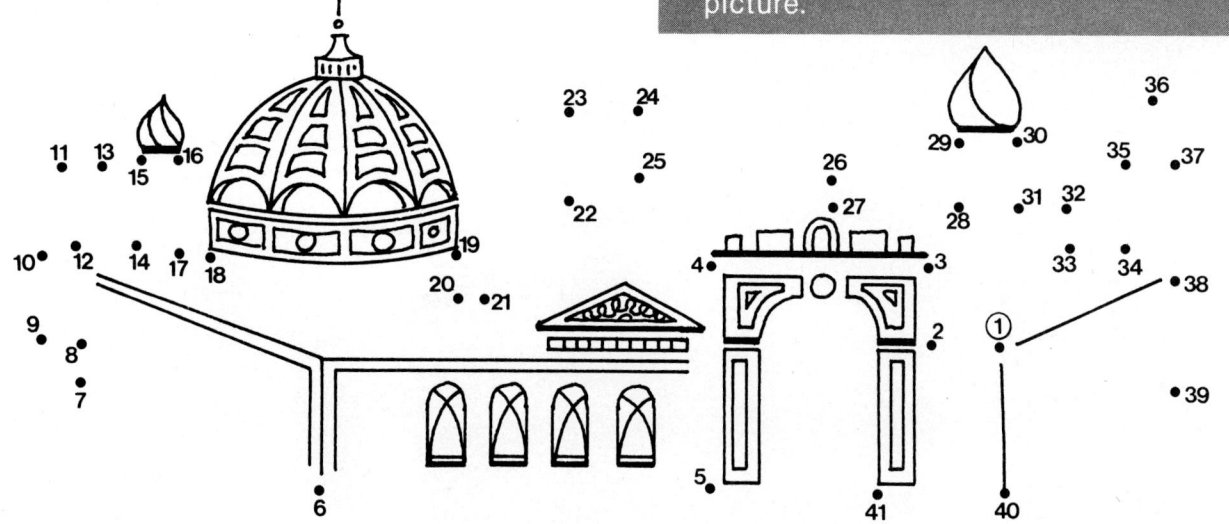

MESSAGES IN CODE

Use this code to find the missing words below. In the boxes, print the letters that match the numbers.

A	B	C	D	E	F
1	2	3	4	5	6

H	I	L	M	N	O
7	8	9	10	11	12

P	R	S	T	U	Y
13	14	15	16	17	18

1. Jesus gave us the eight beatitudes to help us share His ☐☐☐☐☐☐☐☐☐.
   7 1 13 13 8 11 5 15 15

2. People are ☐☐☐☐☐☐☐ when they think that riches will make them happy.
   6 12 12 9 8 15 7

3. Sorrowing people will be ☐☐☐☐☐☐☐☐☐.
   3 12 10 6 12 14 16 5 4

4. Lowly people are gentle and ☐☐☐☐☐☐ of heart.
   7 17 10 2 9 5

5. People who hunger and thirst to be holy ☐☐☐☐☐☐ to please God.
   4 5 15 8 14 5

6. Jesus said, "Be ☐☐☐☐☐☐☐ as your heavenly Father is merciful."
   10 5 14 3 8 6 17 9

7. Peacemakers will be called ☐☐☐☐☐☐☐ of God.
   3 7 8 9 4 14 5 11

8. Jesus said, "They will make you ☐☐☐☐☐☐ for My name."
   15 17 6 6 5 14

169

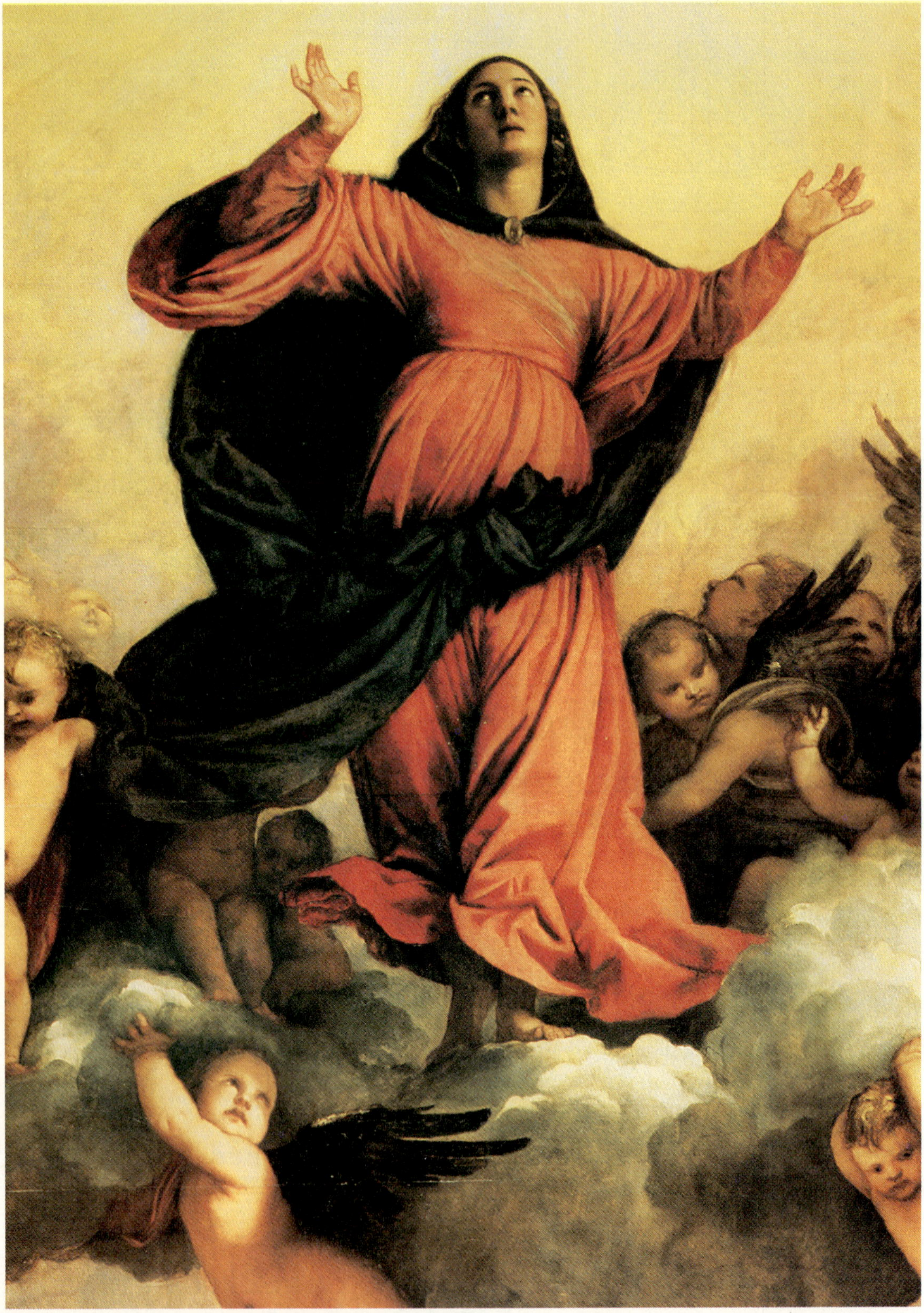

30 WE REJOICE WITH MARY

Mary Is Queen of Heaven and Earth

When Mary died, she was taken body and soul into heavenly glory. Mary shared in the resurrection of Jesus. We call this her "Assumption." In heaven, she now rejoices with the angels and saints. We celebrate Mary's Assumption on August 15.

God made Mary the queen of heaven and earth. He wants Mary to take care of us. She helps us to follow Jesus.

This is why we pray to her. Someday through death we can share in the glory of Jesus' resurrection. Our bodies will be glorified, too. We will be united with Jesus, Mary, the angels, saints and all those we love in heaven.

We celebrate Mary's Assumption on _____
_____
_____.

A SONG TO MARY

Here is a song to Mary, Queen of Heaven and Earth.

Hail, Holy Queen, Enthroned Above

1. Hail, Holy Queen, enthroned above, O Maria!
   Hail, Mother of Mercy and of Love, O Maria!

   Refrain:

   Triumph, all ye cherubim,
   Sing with us, ye seraphim,
   Heav'n and earth resound the hymn:
   Salve, salve, salve Regina!

2. And when our life on earth is done, O Maria!
   Then show us Christ, thy holy Son, O Maria!

WE REMEMBER

Why do we honor Mary?
We honor Mary because
she is the mother of Jesus.
We praise God
for her many gifts.

WE RESPOND

Holy Mary, Mother of God,
pray for us sinners,
now and at the hour
of our death.

We Honor Mary by Many Titles

The Church honors Mary because she is the mother of Jesus. When we honor Mary, we praise God because He gave her so many gifts and graces.

We honor Mary by many titles in the *Litany of Our Lady*. As we say each title to honor her, we think of a special gift God gave her. After we say each title, we ask Mary to pray for us. We want her to ask Jesus for the graces we need to be holy.

From the Litany of Our Lady

Response: **Pray for us.**

Holy Mary,

Holy Mother of God,

Mother of Christ,

Mother most pure,

Mother most merciful,

Virgin most faithful,

Help of Christians,

Queen of apostles and martyrs,

Queen of all saints,

Queen of the most holy rosary,

Queen of peace.

Let us pray:

O God, Giver of all good gifts,

through Mary's prayers for us,

free us from sin and bring us

to eternal happiness.

Through Christ, our Lord.

Amen.

ARE WE ACTING LIKE MARY?

Under each picture, write what you can do to be like Mary.

173

Work the puzzle by using the clues in the lasso.

Down:
2 He was the brother of Andrew
3 People who follow Jesus' way of love
4 The father of those who believe in God
6 Our share in God's life
7 She was called to be Jesus' mother and ours
9 What God calls us to be

Across:
1 What Jesus' beatitudes help us to be
4 Twelve men called by Jesus
5 A king who wrote some psalms
8 What we are because we belong to the Church

GRACE
ABRAHAM
APOSTLE
CHRISTIAN
CATHOLIC
HOLY
DAVID
MARY
PETER
HAPPY

BE A WINNER!

Unscramble the letters and print the word that belongs on each line.

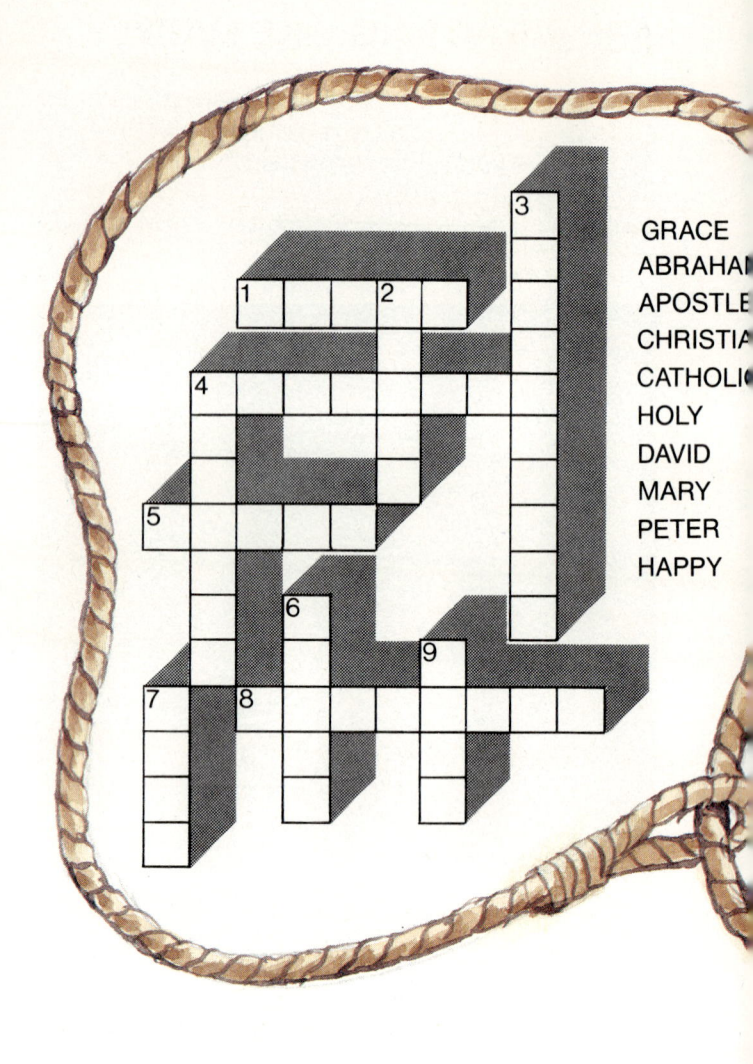

1 Jesus is _____ in the Blessed Sacrament. (rpseent)

2 Parents love us and we should _____ them. (byeo)

3 Sometimes we must suffer for what is _____. (gtrih)

4 Jesus said that we should _____ one another. (olev)

5 In the Sacrament of Reconciliation, Jesus forgives our _____. (nsis)

6 On Sunday we worship God by celebrating _____. (asMs)

7 During vacation we should remember our daily _____. (ryearps)

FOLLOW THE TRAIL TO THE CORRAL

To find the words in the trail, start in the **Open Range** and skip every other letter. Print the word that belongs on each blank below.

Open Range: M K A X S C S O J A E D S J U R S B P N R Y A Z Y K E F R L G H O C D V G R H E W H S T M O G S T J N E K S Z U C S C S B G C P R L A T C F E H S N A F C D R B A J M O E X N S T Y S

1. To celebrate Sunday we take part in _____ _ _ _ _ _____ We bring joy to others.

2. We offer ourselves at Mass with the _____ _ _ _ _ _ _ perfect sacrifice of _____ _ _ _ _

3. _____ is the lifting up of our minds and hearts to God.

4. The first three commandments tell us _____ _ _ _ _ _ _ _ how to love _____

5. The last seven commandments tell us _____ _ _ _ _ _ _ _ _ how to love _____

6. The life of grace was won for us by _____ _ _ _ _ _ _ _ _ _ _ _____

7. The gift by which we share God's life _____ _ _ _ _ _ _ _ _ _ _ _ is _____

8. To meet Jesus and become more like _____ _ _ _ _ _ _ Him, we receive the _____

WE FOLLOW JESUS WITH LOVE

Choose your own answers to complete these sentences.

To show that I love God

I will _____ _ _ _ _ _ _ _ _ _ _ _ _ _ _ _ _ each day.

I will _____ _ _ _ _ _ _ _ _ _ _ _ _ _ _ _ _ every Sunday.

To show that I love my parents and others

I will _____ _ _ _ _ _ _ _ _ _ _ _ _ _ _ _ _ each day.

I will _____ _ _ _ _ _ _ _ _ _ _ _ _ _ _ _ _

175

LITURGY PLANNING SHEET

Group 1: Write Introduction for the Mass

Welcome everyone and tell why you have come to celebrate.

_____

_____

_____

Introduction will be read by _____

Group 2: Select Songs

Choose an entrance song that will give the celebration a good start.

Entrance Song is _____

Choose a song to sing during the Preparation of the Gifts.

Song chosen is _____

Choose to either sing or recite the Our Father _____

Choose a communion song that tells of your joy in being one with Jesus and with others.

Communion Song is _____

Choose a song that thanks God and tells Him how you will try to live the Mass.

Closing Song is _____

Group 3: Prepare the First Reading and the Responses

The First Reading will be _____

It will be read by _____

The Responsorial Psalm will be _____

_____

Alleluia (or Lenten verse) melody will be _____

Holy, Holy, Holy will be _____

We proclaim the Mystery of Faith by _____

The Great Amen will be _____

Group 4:   Compose the Prayer of the Faithful to be Read at Mass

The priest will offer the introductory prayer.

The response to each petition is _____

For the Holy Father, that he _____

_____, we pray to the Lord.

For the Church, that _____

_____, we pray to the Lord.

For our country, that _____

_____, we pray to the Lord.

For _____

_____, we pray to the Lord.

For _____

_____, we pray to the Lord.

The petitions will be read by _____

Group 5:   Prepare the Altar and Gifts

Bread will be brought by _____

The water and wine will be brought by _____

Other offerings of gifts for the Church and the poor will _____

These will be brought by _____

Group 6:   Plan a Thanksgiving after Holy Communion

Decide on a prayer or song with which to praise and thank Jesus for coming to you in Holy Communion. You may read a prayer which you have written or sing a song while performing gestures to help others pray silently during this time.

The Jesse Tree

- Jesus
- Mary
- Joseph
- David
- Joseph
- Moses
- Adam and Eve
- Noah
- Abraham

AN ADVENT PROJECT FOR THE FAMILY

"Advent" means "coming." During Advent, all Christians prepare to celebrate the coming of Jesus, our Savior. Make Advent a time of prayerful waiting for the celebration of Christ's birth by making a family JESSE TREE.

All the decorations on the JESSE TREE remind us of people who waited for the coming of Jesus. The tree is named after a man from Bethlehem. One of Jesse's sons became the most important king of Israel, King David. God had promised that the Savior would belong to the family of King David. As we decorate the JESSE TREE, we remember God's promise to send us a Savior.

Instructions: Carefully tear out the JESSE TREE on page 180. Mount it on stiff paper and hang it where everyone will be reminded to get ready to celebrate Jesus' birthday. You may wish to decorate the tree in one evening, or you may add one decoration each day for nine days.

ADAM AND EVE

God gave Adam and Eve a share in His own divine life. They were very happy until they sinned by disobeying God. But God loved them even after they had sinned. He promised to send a Savior.

Many, many years passed before God our Father sent His Son Jesus into our world as the Savior. But God's wonderful promise began with Adam and Eve, so we put a symbol of them on the JESSE TREE.

Read *Psalm 100* and draw an apple in Adam and Eve's circle on the JESSE TREE.

JOSEPH

Joseph, the man chosen by God to be the foster father of Jesus, belonged to the family of King David. He lived many hundreds of years after King David died. Joseph was a carpenter and made many beautiful things with his hands.

He was a good and holy man. God knew that he would take loving care of Jesus and Mary.

Read *Matthew 1:18-22* and draw a hammer in Joseph's circle on the JESSE TREE.

MARY

When God saw that the time was right to send the Savior to His people, He chose a mother for His Son. Jesus needed a mother to love Him, to take care of Him, and to help Him grow. God chose Mary, a young Jewish woman, to be the mother of Jesus.

God our Father kept the promise He had made to Adam and Eve. On Christmas day, in the little town of Bethlehem, the Savior was born.

Read *Luke 1:26-34* and draw a flower in Mary's circle on the JESSE TREE.

JESUS

Put a large P in the top circle of the JESSE TREE. Cross the P with an X to form ☧ , a symbol for Christ, the Savior. Use your tree to tell the story of those who got ready for the coming of the Lord. Then pray:

Lord Jesus,
You fill our hearts with Your love.
Help us during Advent to bring
Your love and joy to others. Amen.

NOAH

The children of Adam and Eve sinned, too. In fact, so many people sinned that it seemed everyone forgot about loving God.

But God always remembered His promise to Adam and Eve. God told Noah, a good man, that He would send a flood to destroy all the evil in the world. Noah was to build an ark to save himself, his family, and two of every kind of animal on earth. After the flood, God promised Noah that He would never again destroy the earth by such a huge flood. As a sign of His promise, God showed Noah a beautiful rainbow. So, a rainbow and an ark are signs of God's promise and of His love.

Read *Genesis 9:8-17* and draw a rainbow and ark in Noah's circle on the JESSE TREE.

ABRAHAM

Many, many hundreds of years after the flood, God called Abraham to be the father of His chosen people. God told Abraham to leave his home, his country, and the people he loved. In return, God promised to make Abraham the father of many nations. He told him that the children of his family would be as countless as the stars in the sky. Abraham believed God and did as He asked. Abraham became the father of God's chosen people, the Jewish people.

Read *Genesis 15:1-6* and add stars to Abraham's circle on the JESSE TREE.

JOSEPH

While the Jewish people waited for the Savior their family grew in number. One of their members, Jacob, had twelve sons. Jacob's favorite son was Joseph.

Jacob had given Joseph a beautiful coat of many colors. This made Joseph's brothers very jealous, and one day when they were out watching their sheep, they sold Joseph as a slave to some people who were going to Egypt. Jacob was told that a wild animal had killed his son.

In Egypt, God took care of Joseph by making him a friend of Pharaoh, the king. Joseph helped Pharaoh and all the Egyptians when a great famine came over the land. Because Joseph had stored food when the crops were good, he had enough to keep all the Egyptians from starving during this difficult time.

Joseph's father and brothers did not have enough food to eat, for the famine was in their land, too. Jacob sent his sons to get food from Egypt. Joseph was kind to his brothers. He forgave them for selling him as a slave. He told them to bring all their families to Egypt, and that he would see that all of them had enough to eat.

Read *Acts 7:9-14* and draw a coat of many colors in Joseph's circle on the JESSE TREE.

MOSES

Many years after Joseph died, the Pharaoh of Egypt began to fear that the families of Joseph's relatives would become too powerful in his land. So, he made all the Jewish people slaves. For a long, long time God's chosen people lived as slaves in Egypt. Their life was very hard. But God did not forget them. He sent Moses to lead them to freedom. Through Moses, God set His people free. Then He gave Moses laws to guide His people. We call these laws the Ten Commandments.

Read *Deuteronomy 7:6-9* and put the tablets of the Ten Commandments in Moses' circle on the JESSE TREE.

DAVID

Moses led the Jewish people to the land that God had promised to Abraham so many years before. Then God gave the people kings to rule them.

The greatest king was David. As a boy, David had been a shepherd in the fields of Bethlehem. As a king, David was good and wise. God promised David that the Savior would belong to his family.

Read *Acts 13:22-23* and draw a crown in David's circle on the JESSE TREE.

Sharing Lent as a Family

During Lent we should recall our own Baptism and renew our Christian life. The Church urges us to spend time each day considering the mystery of God's love, as shown especially in the suffering, death, and resurrection of Jesus. To help you make these weeks of Lent a time of spiritual growth, we suggest the following activities.

ASH WEDNESDAY

Talk about what you as a family can do to make each day of Lent a special time for following Christ. Then provide small pieces of paper and ask family members to write down one thing they would like to improve on or eliminate from their lives. On the other side of the paper slip, write your name. After Lent, these slips may be returned so that you can evaluate how well you kept your promises.

THE PRETZEL

The pretzel is made from flour, water, and salt. It reminds us that a long time ago, people fasted from milk, butter, eggs, cheese, cream, and meat during Lent. They made the small breads in the form of arms crossed in prayer which we call pretzels. Serve this special Lenten food during the days of Lent as a reminder that each day should be one of prayer, as well as of fasting.

HOLY THURSDAY

Make Holy Thursday a day of loving self-giving as you recall Christ's complete offering of Himself on Calvary and in the Holy Eucharist.

The Holy Thursday meal can recall the Passover that led to freedom from slavery. Many simplified versions of this ceremonial dinner, known as the "Seder supper," are available for families to use. Plan to attend the parish Holy Thursday evening liturgy as a family.

GOOD FRIDAY

Make a worship center by setting up a crucifix in an appropriate place. Let the children place some sign of their appreciation for Christ's love near the crucifix. The "sign" can be: toys which they will not play with for the sacred three hours of Good Friday, a letter written to the Lord, or a container that has the mission money gathered from all the sacrifices they made during Lent.

If possible, attend the Good Friday liturgy to express love for Jesus Who showed His great love for us on the day He died.

EASTER VIGIL

Easter is not simply one feast among many. It is THE feast of the year and can be truly celebrated as such by those who have prepared their hearts during Lent. Decorate your table with a baptismal robe and candle. Renew your baptismal promises as a family. Talk about the paschal candle that will be seen in church at Mass during the Easter season. Try to be present at the parish celebration of the Easter Vigil.

READING THE BIBLE

Daily Scripture reading can help you form your priorities and attitudes as you come to better understand the Lord's love for you. As you pick up your family Bible, make a triple Sign of the Cross on your forehead, lips and heart, praying as you do so: "The Lord be in my thoughts, on my lips, and in my heart." Invite the children to repeat it after you. Read the Gospel for the next day's Mass and discuss what the Lord is asking you to do to bring His message to the people you meet each day.

Conclude your discussion with the words the Israelites used when Moses gave them the Word of the Lord: "All that the Lord has said, we will do." *(Adapted from Exodus 24:7)* Then reverently place the Bible in its special place, saying, "Happy are those who hear the Word of God and keep it."

SACRIFICE

"Sacrifice," a word commonly associated with Lent, is derived from two Latin words that mean "to make holy." A prayerful reflection and family discussion of *Isaiah 58:1-9* can help your family decide how you can respond more fully to the Lord with Lenten sacrifices. If money is saved, it can be given to relieve social injustices. Many families eat a "poverty meal" once a week during Lent and donate the savings from this meal together with their other Lenten sacrifices to groups devoted to the missions or to the liberation of the poor and powerless.

THE ROSARY

Pray at least one of the sorrowful mysteries each day. As a family, reflect on how our thoughtless treatment of others continues the suffering of Christ even today. Then pray the decade, asking our Blessed Mother's help in overcoming those faults and sins which hurt others.

WAY OF THE CROSS

Follow Christ's way of love by going from station to station in church, or meditate on each station in your own home. Specific prayers are not required when we make the Way of the Cross. Simply reflect upon Jesus' journey of love. (Pictures in booklets can help children become familiar with the stations.)

When contemplating on the stations, discuss what happened at each station, what it tells us about Jesus' love, and how the difficulties you experience each day are related to the sufferings of Jesus. End each meditation with a prayer for help to follow Christ's way of love.

Making Holy Week Special

PASSION SUNDAY (Palm Sunday)

The palms we receive in church on the last Sunday of Lent remind us that when Christ our King entered Jerusalem, the people acclaimed Him and waved palms in welcome. Have a procession during which you place blessed palms in each room of your home. Say as you do so, "Praise and honor to You, Lord Jesus Christ, King of endless glory." Have your family repeat the acclamation. End your procession with a discussion of what your family will do to celebrate Holy Week.

All for You Most Sacred Heart of Jesus

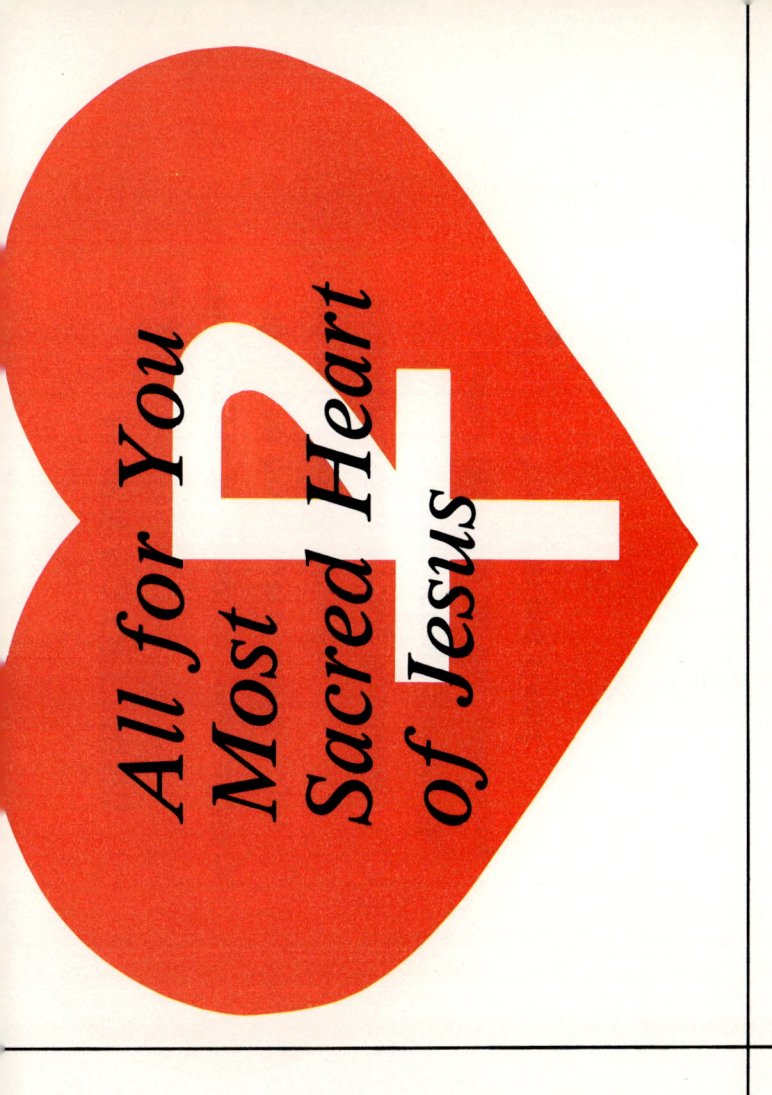

DIRECTIONS

Remove the page by tearing along the broken lines.

Cut apart the cards at the lower half of the page by cutting on the solid lines.

Cut out the heart in the upper half of the page.

Staple or glue the heart to one end of a drinking straw.

Poke a hole in the bottom of a paper cup and push the other end of the straw into it.

BE AN APOSTLE OF PRAYER

Offer your love to Jesus each day by praying the Morning Offering.
Offer all you do during the day as an intention for Jesus.

Pray for all Apostles of Prayer.

Make a special card to help you remember to pray. Directions for this are on the back of this page. Give away the two prayer cards at the bottom of this page.

MORNING OFFERING

O Jesus, through the Immaculate Heart of Mary, I offer You my prayers, works, joys, and sufferings of this day in union with the Holy Sacrifice of the Mass throughout the world. I offer them for all the intentions of Your Sacred Heart. Amen.

MORNING OFFERING

O Jesus,

through the Immaculate

Heart of Mary, I offer You

my prayers, works, joys,

and sufferings of this day

in union with the Holy

Sacrifice of the Mass

throughout the world.

I offer them for all the

intentions of Your

Sacred Heart.

Amen.

♥

MORNING OFFERING

O Jesus,

through the Immaculate

Heart of Mary, I offer You

my prayers, works, joys,

and sufferings of this day

in union with Holy

Sacrifice of the Mass

throughout the world.

I offer them for all the

intentions of Your

Sacred Heart.

Amen.

♥

THIRD SORROWFUL MYSTERY: THE CROWNING WITH THORNS **3**

After the scourging, the soldiers make fun of Jesus. They put a purple robe on Him and crown Him with thorns. They mock Him by saying, "Hail, King of the Jews!" Jesus does not say a word.

Let us ask Jesus to help us be kind to those who hurt us.

Prayers for the Rosary

APOSTLES' CREED

I believe in God, the Father almighty, creator of heaven and earth. I believe in Jesus Christ, his only Son, our Lord. He was conceived by the power of the Holy Spirit and born of the Virgin Mary. He suffered under Pontius Pilate, was crucified, died, and was buried. He descended to the dead. On the third day he rose again. He ascended into heaven, and is seated at the right hand of the Father. He will come again to judge the living and the dead. I believe in the Holy Spirit, the holy catholic Church, the communion of saints, the forgiveness of sins, the resurrection of the body, and life everlasting.
Amen.

OUR FATHER

HAIL MARY

DOXOLOGY

FIFTH SORROWFUL MYSTERY: THE DEATH OF OUR LORD **5**

Jesus suffers for three long hours on the Cross. He forgives His enemies and gives us His mother. He gives up His so that we can live with Him forever.

Let us thank Jesus for His great love and promise to show more love for Him.

My Rosary Book

The Sorrowful Mysteries

FIRST SORROWFUL MYSTERY: THE AGONY IN THE GARDEN

After the Last Supper, Jesus goes to the garden to pray. Peter, James, and John go with Him. While Jesus prays, He suffers a bloody sweat. He offers His sufferings for our sins.

Let us tell Jesus how sorry we are for our sins.

SECOND SORROWFUL MYSTERY: THE SCOURGING

Because Pilate is afraid of the people, he has Jesus scourged, or whipped. The soldiers whip Jesus with heavy cords. Jesus suffers this for our sins.

Let us ask Jesus to help us accept little pains as a way to make up for sin.

FOURTH SORROWFUL MYSTERY: THE CARRYING OF THE CROSS

Jesus carries the heavy cross because He loves us. How sad it is when He meets His mother on the way! Jesus is so weak that He falls three times.

Let us ask Jesus to help us be brave when we have something difficult to do.

FOURTH GLORIOUS MYSTERY: THE ASSUMPTION

After Jesus' death, Mary helps the apostles for many years. When her life on earth ends, Jesus takes her, body and soul, into heaven. He does this because He loves His mother very much. She has never sinned.

Let us ask Mary to help us so that we may one day share in her glory.

FIRST GLORIOUS MYSTERY: THE RESURRECTION

Jesus rises from the dead on the third day. He is seen by His mother, by Mary Magdalene, and by the apostles. To the apostle Thomas He says, "Blessed are they who believe and have not seen."

Let us tell Jesus that we believe in Him.

Color a bead each time you say your prayers.

My Rosary Book

The Glorious Mysteries

SECOND GLORIOUS MYSTERY: THE ASCENSION

Before Jesus ascends into heaven, He tells His apostles to teach the Good News and baptize people everywhere. He tells them to wait for the Holy Spirit. Then He ascends into heaven to prepare a place for everyone.

Let us tell Jesus that we hope to live with Him in heaven some day.

THIRD GLORIOUS MYSTERY: THE COMING OF THE HOLY SPIRIT

Mary and the disciples wait and pray for the Holy Spirit to come. When He comes, tongues of fire can be seen above the head of each of them. He fills their hearts with great love.

Let us ask the Holy Spirit to make our love stronger.

Prayers for the Rosary

APOSTLES' CREED

I believe in God, the Father almighty, creator of heaven and earth. I believe in Jesus Christ, his only Son, our Lord. He was conceived by the power of the Holy Spirit and born of the Virgin Mary. He suffered under Pontius Pilate, was crucified, died, and was buried. He descended to the dead. On the third day he rose again. He ascended into heaven, and is seated at the right hand of the Father. He will come again to judge the living and the dead. I believe in the Holy Spirit, the holy catholic Church, the communion of saints, the forgiveness of sins, the resurrection of the body, and life everlasting. Amen.

OUR FATHER

HAIL MARY

DOXOLOGY

FIFTH GLORIOUS MYSTERY: THE CROWNING OF MARY

Jesus honors Mary in heaven. She is crowned Queen of Heaven and Earth. She watches over us and prays for us.

Let us ask Mary to help us grow in love for Jesus.

ACT OF CONTRITION

My God, I am sorry for my sins with all my heart. In choosing to do wrong and failing to do good, I have sinned against you whom I should love above all things. I firmly intend, with your help, to do penance, to sin no more, and to avoid whatever leads me to sin.

Our Savior Jesus Christ suffered and died for us. In his name, my God, have mercy.

God Forgives Me

If we tell our sins, Jesus can be trusted to forgive them.

Adapted from 1 John 1:9

How good God is!
With all my heart and soul and strength I want to tell Him so. I do not forget His goodness to me. He forgives me and makes me strong again. He has redeemed my life.

Adapted from Psalm 103:1-5

As I look at Jesus nailed to the Cross, I feel sorry for having sinned. I think about how I have failed to show love to God and others.

I Finish My Confession

The priest may talk to me about how to be more loving. He gives me a penance. Then I tell God I am sorry in an Act of Contrition.

The priest may say, "Give thanks to the Lord for He is good."

I respond: His mercy endures forever.

I Thank God

I will give thanks to You, O Lord, with all my heart.

Adapted from Psalm 138:1

Thank You, dear God, for Your love and goodness to me. Thank You for Your peace and fatherly forgiveness.

I will bring peace to others and try to love them more.

I will try to be more like Jesus each day.
Mother Mary, pray for me.
Holy Spirit, help me.
Amen.

I do the penance the priest gives me.

CONFESSION BOOKLET ✢

"My Peace
I give
to you."

This booklet belongs to

I Examine My Conscience

HOW MUCH DO I LOVE GOD?

- Do I pray to God? How often?

- Do I use God's name with love? Have I used His name in the wrong way?

- Do I celebrate Sunday by assisting at Saturday evening or Sunday Mass? Have I missed Sunday Mass deliberately?

- Do I listen well to God's Word?

- Do I thank God for His goodness to me?

- Do I tell God I am sorry when I have failed to love?

- Do I ask God to help me?

- Have I really been the person Jesus expects me to be?

HOW MUCH DO I LOVE OTHERS?

- Do I listen to and obey those who care for me?

- Am I kind and loving to my family and others? Have I hurt anyone? Do I make up with those I hurt? Do I call others bad names or make fun of them? Was I too selfish to share things with others or to help them? Do I show respect for myself and others?

- Have I been pure in my thoughts, words, and actions? Do I choose good friends? Am I faithful to them? Have I looked at only good movies, TV shows, pictures and books?

- Am I careful not to waste God's gifts so that other people can enjoy them? Am I satisfied with what I have? Do I share with people in need? Am I honest? Have I taken something that was not mine? Did I return it? Did I damage anyone's property? Did I pay for or repair what I damaged?

- Did I lie to anyone? Did I talk about others in an unkind way? Have I kept promises and secrets?

PRAYER TO THE HOLY SPIRIT

Come, Holy Spirit,
fill the hearts of
Your faithful,
and kindle in them
the fire of Your love.

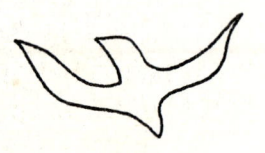

Holy Spirit,
Help me to know
how I have loved.
Help me to know
how I have
failed to love.
Help me to be
sorry for failing
to love.
Help me to trust
in God's loving
forgiveness.
Amen.

I Make My Confession

The priest welcomes me and I greet him.

I make the Sign of the Cross.

The priest says a prayer to help me remember God's forgiving love.

I say, "AMEN."

The priest may read God's Word from the Bible. I listen.

I make my confession. I may begin by saying:

"FORGIVE ME, FATHER,
I have sinned. My last confession was _____ ago."

When I am finished telling my sins, I may say, "I AM SORRY FOR ALL MY SINS."